Economic Dependency in Africa and Latin America

BARB

Stanfo

S

Printed in the United States of America

For information address:

SAGE PUBLICATIONS, INC.
275 South Beverly Drive
Beverly Hills, California 90212

SAGE PUBLICATIONS LTD
St George's House / 44 Hatton Garden
London E C 1

International Standard Book Number 0-8039-0149-6

Library of Congress Catalog Card No. 72-84039

SECOND PRINTING

CONTENTS

Economic Overview 9

Foreign Capital Flow 13

Trade 26

Foreign Manpower 31

Conclusions 35

Notes 44

References 48

Appendix 54

LIST OF TABLES

Table 1 Economic Indicators for African, Latin American, and Major Donor Countries, 1965 8
Table 2 Estimated Accumulated Direct Investment by OECD Members in Less-Developed Countries as of December 1966 14
Table 3 Net Bilateral Aid by Major Donors, 1960-1967 16
Table 4 Net Multilateral Aid by Donors, 1960-1967 18
Table 5 Aid Concentration, 1967 20
Table 6 Gross Inflow of Foreign Capital by Types, 1960-1967 22
Table 7 Net Inflow of Foreign Capital, 1960-1967 23
Table 8 Destination of Exports, 1960-1966 24
Table 9 Origin of Imports, 1960-1966 25
Table 10 Trade Concentration, 1967 28
Table 11 Export Commodity Concentration, 1967 30
Table 12 Bilateral Technical Assistance, 1965 32
Table 13 Importance of Foreign Training, 1963 33
Table 14 Index of Immigration of Professional and Technical Workers into the United States, 1964-1969 34
Table 15 Personnel (excluding teachers) Supplied by OECD Bilateral Technical Assistance, 1963 35
Table 16 Public Debt Service and Investment Income Payment as Percentage of Exports, 1967 or 1968 42
Appendix. Indicators for African, Latin American, and Major Donor Countries, 1965 54

Economic Dependency in Africa and Latin America

BARBARA STALLINGS
Stanford University

One of the most important developments in the study of Third World countries is the recent emergence of what has been called dependency theory.[1] This approach, developed mostly by Latin American social scientists,[2] owes its largest debt to the work of Marx and Lenin on the international capitalist system in general and on imperialism in particular. In a sense, dependency theory can be seen as an attempt to look at imperialism from the bottom up rather than from the top down; that is, to look at the effects on the exploited countries (Third World) instead of the exploiters (industrialized nations). In essence, the theory is an explanation for the *failure* of Third World countries to develop.[3]

Although there is a good deal of disagreement among those working on the concept of dependency,[4] and although the theory itself is far from fully developed, it is possible to indicate the basic ideas involved. A thumbnail sketch is provided by Chilean economist Osvaldo Sunkel (and Paz, 1970: 37; my translation):

> It does not view development as a "moment" in the continuous or discontinuous evolution of a society which is economically, politically and culturally isolated. On the contrary, it postulates . . . that underdevelopment is part of the global historical process of development, and that development and underdevelopment are two faces of the same universal historical process. Both processes occur simultaneously, and they are linked functionally; that is, they

---

AUTHOR'S NOTE: *The author would like to thank Professors Richard Fagen and David Abernethy for comments on earlier drafts of this paper.*

> interact and mutually influence each other. The concrete geographical expression of the relationship can be observed in two great dualisms: on the one hand, the division of the world *between* advanced, developed, industrialized, center states and underdeveloped, backward, poor, peripheral, dependent states; and, on the other hand, the division *within* states in regions, social groups, and activities which are modern and advanced and regions, groups and activities which are backward, primitive and dependent.

As this description indicates, there are many questions to be examined with regard to dependency. One set of questions involves the *inter*national relationships between advanced and underdeveloped countries. Another set concerns *intra*national relations between different classes and regions within the underdeveloped countries themselves. Cutting across these two divisions, we must consider the economic, political, and cultural aspects of both the international and the intranational linkages. Finally, it must be understood that all these relationships have changed over time and are still changing according to structural changes in the nations involved.[5] Although all these topics, as well as the interactions among them, are extremely important for understanding what is happening in the Third World today, only one aspect can be covered in this paper. Here the primary emphasis will be on international economic relations.

Perhaps at this point it would be helpful to attempt a rough definition of what is meant in this paper by economic dependency for, of course, no country can be completely independent in the twentieth century. A dependent nation (economically speaking) is one which does not have control over the major decisions affecting its own economy. A corollary of this definition is that there is a concentration of this control in one or several advanced nations. To give just one example of the difference between dependence (condition of the underdeveloped countries) and interdependence (condition of the developed countries); most of the underdeveloped countries depend for a majority of their exports and imports on one single advanced nation, while that nation, in turn, does only a small amount of its trade with the underdeveloped country. This would be one aspect of dependency with respect to trade. Interdependency, on the other hand, might be exemplified by an industrialized country which trades with many countries (in this respect, it is not totally independent), but only a small portion of its trade is carried on with any one nation. A second corollary is that, since the advanced countries make the decisions, the benefits from the economic relationships between the dominant and the dominated nations accrue disproportionately to the former, thus increasing their economic capacity at the expense of the Third World countries. This is what Sunkel referred to when he said that development and underdevelopment are two faces of the same historical process.

Operationally speaking, economic dependency is seen here in terms of

(1) concentration of imported capital—"aid" and private investment—from a few advanced countries;
(2) concentration of trade with a limited number of industrialized countries with the underdeveloped countries supplying mainly primary products; and
(3) concentration of foreign personnel from a few advanced nations.[6]

The obvious implication is that the more these three conditions exist, the greater the potential influence of an advanced nation in the affairs of any given Third World country. That this potential influence has been used in many and varied ways is well documented.[7] The most important aspect is the concentration factor. Whatever the amount of foreign participation in the economy, it is difficult to relinquish it, in part because of the internal relationships to be discussed below. When one advanced country alone controls this flow of capital, trade, and personnel, then dependency is at its height.

Although the same underlying forces of economic dependency have been operating throughout the Third World since initial contact with the now advanced nations, certain historical factors, as well as natural resource endowments, have meant that the process has moved at different rates and appeared in slightly different forms in each individual country. Although this means that ultimately we need to look at the pattern of dependency in each country, there are certain similarities within regions as wholes which it may be helpful to trace before looking at individual cases. Regional differences may be caused by many factors. Two of the most important are the particular country(ies) which is(are) dominating the region, and the amount of time the region has been politically independent. The largest differences are probably between Latin America and tropical Africa.[8] By comparing these two regions, we may get a somewhat better idea of the various faces and problems of economic dependency. In addition, because Latin America has been involved in the process of dependent development longer, it may have certain "lessons" to offer Africa and the rest of the Third World as these nations now try to develop.

There are, then, three purposes to this paper: the first is to present some data on economic dependency—a concept which thus far has largely lacked an empirical base; the second is to compare Latin America and

TABLE 1

Economic Indicators for African, Latin American, and Major Donor Countries, 1965[a]

Indicator	Africa	Latin America	Major Donors[b]
Economic Capacity			
GNP per capita	$104 ($41-$356)	$296 ($87-$874)	$1,870 ($1,382-$3,482)
Agriculture as % of GDP	47% (10%- 69%)	28% (10%-49%)	5% (3%-22%)
Industry as % of GDP	7% (1%- 19%)	21% (15%-40%)	41% (34%-52%)
Infrastructure			
Railroad miles/sq. miles	3.2 mi. (0-12.9 mi.)	16.2 mi. (1.5-481.2 mi.)	96.8 mi. (9.4-229.0 mi.)
Energy consumption per capita	44 kg (10-487 kg)	326 kg (33-2974 kg)	4234 kg (2951-9201 kg)
Educational Level			
% literate	10% (3%- 41%)	65% (10%-91%)	99% (–)
University students/1,000 population	1/10,000 (0-11/10,000)	31/10,000 (4-109/10,000)	104/10,000 (49-284/10,000)
Growth Rates			
GNP growth rate[c]	3.1% (0.9%-8.9%)	4.7% (–0.1%-8.3%)	4.7% (3.3%-6.4%)
GNP per capita growth rate[c]	0.9% (–1.6%-6.9%)	1.5% (–1.7%-4.7%)	3.4% (2.5%-5.0%)
Size of Market			
Population	3.7 mil (0.5-57.5 mil)	4.4 mil (1.3-82.2 mil)	59.0 mil (48.9-230.6 mil)
% of countries with population >10 million	17%	25%	100%
% of population in cities over 50,000	4% (0%- 24%)	24% (6%-50%)	36% (25%-49%)
Importance of Foreign Sector			
Trade as % of GNP	43% (20%-121%)	29% (12%-54%)	22% (7%-31%)
Foreign capital as % of gross investment[d]	22%	8%	0%
Distribution			
Gini index (income)[e]	.48 (.31-.64)	.50 (.32-.62)	.45 (.40-.52)
Gini index (land)	.59 (.48-.69)	.83 (.69-.93)	.71 (.67-.72)

SOURCE: See appendix except for "foreign capital as % of gross investment," which is taken from Lester Pearson et al. (1969: 31).

a. Figures are median and range unless otherwise specified.

b. France, Germany (West), Soviet Union, United Kingdom, and United States.

c. Period covered is 1960-1965.

d. Mean for 1960-1967.

e. Mean.

tropical Africa with respect to these data; and the third is to discuss some of the implications of the comparisons.

One cautionary note should be added. The paper relies heavily on aggregate data. The problems with this type of research are well known, even for advanced nations with adequate statistical series (probably the best article on general problems of aggregate data is still Scheuch, 1966). Problems with data from Third World countries are much greater. Therefore, the data which are presented should be read not as absolute figures but only as general approximations. (This should not cause too much trouble since most of the differences between Africa and Latin America are quite large.) When data sources are especially inadequate, this will be noted in the text.

ECONOMIC OVERVIEW

Any examination of recent data on Africa and Latin America reinforces the idea of Africa's backwardness with respect to economic capacity. That is, not only is Africa underdeveloped in comparison with the major industrialized countries, it is also underdeveloped in comparison with other parts of the Third World.

Table 1 compares the two regions (and the major donor countries) on several dimensions–economic capacity, infrastructure, education, growth rates, size of the potential market, importance of the foreign sector, and distribution. (Detailed information from which this summary table was drawn can be found in the appendix.) In general, these figures are given in terms of the median and the range, and while it can be seen that the medians are quite different, it should also be noted that there is a good deal of overlap on almost all the indicators as seen by looking at the range data. In other words, the poorest Latin American countries are invariably worse off than the richest African ones.

Looking first at the figures for per capita GNP, it can be seen that the median figure for Latin America is almost three times as high as that for Africa, and that the highest African figure is only $356. These disparities are relevant not only as they illuminate the differences in material benefits available, but also because GNP data tend to be correlated with other kinds of statistics which are relevant for development. This can be clearly seen in Table 1, with the data on infrastructure and educational level. In each case, these latter figures bear out the fact of Latin America's higher level of economic capacity. The indicators of transportation capacity (railroad miles per square mile) and energy consumption (kg. per capita of coal equivalent) are important both as indicators and by themselves. Railroad-building, for instance, has traditionally been one of the main stimulants of growth (although Kamarck, 1971: 219, says that trucks and even airlines are taking over this role in Africa). Energy production is likewise vitally necessary for economic growth as well as individual consumption. The statistics for both these dimensions show Latin America to be several times better off than Africa but, of course, far behind the advanced countries.

Trained personnel are also essential to development; the two indicators in Table 1 show different kinds of "expertise." First is the percentage of the population which is literate and therefore possesses the minimum qualifications necessary for skilled labor. At the other end of the spectrum is the need for technicians and professionals usually produced by university education. Although Africa may have less than one-sixth as many literate citizens as are found in Latin America, it is even worse off with respect to university students, having only one student for every 10,000 population while Latin America has 31 per 10,000.

Other data in Table 1 have to do with what might be called growth *potential,* rather than actual growth. For example, the relative importance of agriculture and manufacturing in the GDP (agriculture representing 47% in Africa as opposed to 28% in Latin America, while industry contributes 7% in the former and 21% in the latter) is significant since agriculture has traditionally had a lower level of productivity and grown at a much slower rate than industry.[9] This means that one would expect that countries highly dependent on agriculture would grow at a slower rate (though the reverse does not necessarily hold). This may be one explanation for the fact that Latin America has had a higher growth rate, both in the aggregate and per capita, in recent years. During the early 1960s, the Latin American per capita GNP averaged a 1.5% annual increase, while Africa grew at only 0.9% a year.

Another factor bearing on growth potential is the size of the countries. The median population of the African countries is 3.7 million, while Latin America's median is slightly higher at 4.4 million. Only 17% of African nations and 25% of Latin American nations have populations above ten million, which might provide an internal market adequate, at least, for intermediate-level industry. This means that unless some kind of regional integration scheme is negotiated, it is very unlikely that efficient heavy industry can be established in the majority of the countries under consideration. In Africa, of course, the current situation is even worse because such a large percentage of the population is outside the money economy. Although not really an adequate indicator of the latter, the percentage of the population living in urban areas (4% in Africa and 24% in Latin America) gives some idea of the difference in this respect.

One final item which can be illustrated by the data in Table 1 is the relative importance of the outside world in the economies of the two regions. Trade, for instance (as measured by exports plus imports divided by the GNP), is more important to Africa than to Latin America, representing 43% of GNP in the former and only 29% in the latter. (It should be noted that dependence on trade is less an indicator of underdevelopment than of size; that is, even the smaller industrialized nations are highly dependent on trade.) Even greater differences are found with regard to the role of foreign capital, which represents 22% of gross investment in Africa and only 8% in Latin America.

Data on the importance of foreign personnel are not given in Table 1, but a rough idea can be obtained from the fact that foreign manpower provided by technical assistance and foreign investment composes about 0.5% of high-level skills in Brazil and about 1% in Mexico, while these sources provide the majority of highly skilled manpower in black Africa (Maddison, 1965: 19-20). No data are available for Latin America as a whole, though the figure is certainly higher than for Brazil and Mexico. Another report adds that while OECD bilateral technical assistance provides about 1% of university professors in developing countries as a whole (again, no breakdown for Latin America separately), three-fourths of university faculty in Africa come from this source (Kamarck, 1971: 258 fn.).

Although Africa is quite apparently "worse off" from the point of view of economic capacity, this backwardness is nevertheless accompanied by some advantages from the point of view of change. Specifically, class and interest group structures are less developed, which means that there are fewer forces with an interest in preserving the status quo. (The tribal structure in Africa may, of course, tend to offset this advantage.)

There are some data on income distribution given in Table 1, but it is unclear as to how comparable they really are because of different methods of measurement. These data are an overall measure of distribution as given by gini indices. The same relationships can be seen, however, by looking at the share of the bottom 20 or 40% of the population or at the top 5%. All three measures show African countries with a more equal distribution than Latin America. The land distribution data point in this same direction also, although the latter comparison should not be taken too seriously since the data on Africa are based on only two countries (Kenya and Mali). In addition to quantitative data, qualitative information also reinforces the idea of greater equality in Africa than in Latin America. One comparative evaluation is from Gerald Helleiner (1971:93):

> Policies relating to distribution are essential in the 1970's if Africa is not to recreate the Latin American development pattern. The rigidity of the social structure characteristic of Latin America . . . does not yet curse the tropical African scene. This is not to say that the traditional authority structure and ethnic loyalties are unimportant or that there exist no social or economic classes. One does sense, however, a much greater social malleability, at least in the monetized sectors of the economy. The social divisions in most of tropical Africa have not hardened.

A similar situation can be found with interest groups, primarily because such a large percentage of the population in Africa is still engaged in subsistence agriculture, a group which is practically impossible to organize. Those farmers engaged in growing crops for the domestic—and especially the export—market, such as the Ashanti cocoa farmers in Ghana, are more easily organized. Worker organization in Africa then is basically confined to urban unions, but they are already tending to increase wages to the point of exhausting scarce resources and therefore limiting other development possibilities (Robson and Lury, 1969: 61-62). Since there is so little industry, entrepreneurs are less important in Africa than in Latin America, but the one elite group which cannot be forgotten is the bureaucrats who enjoy large salaries and other privileges as part of the colonial legacy (Kamarck, 1971: 74-75).

In Latin America, on the other hand, both employees and employers tend to be organized, in rural as well as urban areas. In Brazil, for instance, approximately 40% of the urban workers were members of unions in 1960, and 10 other Latin American nations had higher trade union densities than Brazil. In addition to workers, over 20% of industrial employers were organized and about 12% of rural landowners (Schmitter, 1971: 159-160). Both the employer and employee organizations are very influential in government policy in most Latin American countries.

One final point on which it is hard to obtain adequate quantitative data is the degree to which the governments in the two areas are able to extract resources from their citizens. If a government is to rely on its own resources rather than external help, it must be able to extract those resources. One possible indicator is the ratio of income tax revenue to total domestic revenue. Data available for 15 African and 19 Latin American countries show no difference on this dimension. The median ratio for Africa is 17.2% and for Latin America it is 17.3%. The median for donor countries is 55.0%.[10] Unfortunately, this information does not distinguish between personal and corporate income tax so that, in some countries, the money is coming from a few large extractive or other industries, and, in others, from more average citizens. Of course, the ability to extract *any* kind of taxes is important. Perhaps a logical assumption would be that government extractive ability is probably somewhat greater in Latin America than in Africa, if only because of the high percentage of the population in subsistence agriculture in Africa. (The similar figures for income tax percentages may derive from the fact that data are available for only half the African countries, and those which have no data probably have lower rates of tax collection also.) On the other hand, the more rigid class structure in Latin America makes taxing the wealthy very difficult.

FOREIGN CAPITAL FLOW

The most obvious aspect of economic dependency is reliance on foreign capital. Three types of external capital flow are important in considering the relative positions of Africa and Latin America: private foreign investment, bilateral government aid, and aid from multilateral organizations. Private foreign investment is of two main kinds–portfolio investment (such as bonds) and direct investment (ownership of physical assets). The former was originally more important, but, since World War II, direct foreign investment has become predominant. It is difficult to obtain exact figures on the amount of direct foreign investment because only the United States keeps such statistics on its nationals. The OECD, however, has estimated that its members[11] had invested a total of almost $30 billion in the less-developed countries as of the end of 1966. Table 2 shows the breakdown for Africa and Latin America by sectors. As can be seen, investment in Africa totalled $4.9 billion (16.4% of total investment in developing countries) and in Latin America $15.7 billion (52.2%). These figures must be modified, however, as the African totals include North Africa (though excluding South Africa). My estimate would be that at least one-half the African investment is found in North Africa, so that actually Latin America has between five and six times as much private investment as black Africa. The sectoral breakdowns are as would be expected: Africa has more than its percentage share in the extractive sectors (mining and petroleum), while Latin America is overrepresented in manufacturing.

If data in general on private investment are difficult to find, precise trend data are even more scarce. Nevertheless, the general pattern of foreign investment is fairly clear. Foreign investment in Latin America has been present since the sixteenth century–first dominated by Spain and Portugal in the colonial period, then by the British from the time of

TABLE 2
Estimated Accumulated Direct Investment by OECD Members in Less-Developed Countries as of December 1966 (millions of U.S. dollars)

	Region		
	Africa	Latin America	Total for Less-Developed Countries
Petroleum	2,041 (17.1)[a]	4,878 (41.0)	11,892 (100.0)
Mining and smelting	792 (28.7)	1,697 (61.6)	2,751 (100.0)
Manufacturing	,806 (9.9)	5,261 (64.9)	8,097 (100.0)
Other	1,277 (17.6)	3,828 (52.9)	7,230 (100.0)
Total	4,916 (16.4)	15,664 (52.2)	29,970 (100.0)

SOURCE: Pearson et al. (1969: 376).
a. Percentages in parentheses.

independence early in the nineteenth century, and finally taken over by the United States after World War I. U.S. investment currently accounts for between two-thirds and three-fourths of all foreign investment in Latin America (and, correspondingly, Latin America represents about 20% of all U.S. foreign investment). Other major investors are Germany, Japan, Italy, and the United Kingdom to a lesser extent (OECD, geographical distribution, 1960-1964, 1965, 1966-1967). As far as types of investment go, these trends are also fairly clear. Early investment was primarily in infrastructure and public utilities—railroads, banks, electricity, telephone companies, and the like—and extractive industries. There was also some investment in agriculture, especially in Central America. Now many of the former areas have been bought out by the countries involved (often to the great relief of the foreign corporations concerned, since infrastructure investment is not very profitable), and investment has been transferred to the more dynamic manufacturing sector. Oil and mining investments are becoming more closed to foreign investment, and profits have also decreased as governments raised taxes. Very little outright nationalization has taken place and, with the exception of Cuba, adequate compensation has been worked out with the companies involved.[12]

Africa, on the other hand, has a much shorter history of foreign investment. There was little investment prior to World War I, and what there was was done by chartered companies, most of which went bankrupt and were taken over by the governments involved. As might be expected, most private investment in the various African countries was owned by nationals of the colony's mother country; thus, British companies invested in British colonies, and so on. After World War II, U.S. corporations began investing in Africa, and, more recently, German investment has become significant again (see Kamarck, 1971: 238-249 for a general history of foreign investment in Africa; for more recent developments, see Seidman, 1970). Sectoral trend data are available only for U.S. investment which may not be representative of other countries. These data (for black Africa only) show that petroleum was most important in the 1950s (representing 41% of U.S. investment), followed by mining (34%), and agriculture (21%). By 1966, petroleum had become even more dominant (52%), mining remained about the same (37%), while agricultural investment almost disappeared (representing less than 1%). Manufacturing investment increased over this period from less than 1% to over 5%.[13] A few of the African countries, notably Tanzania, Zambia, and Guinea, have attempted to control or take over some private foreign investment.

Bilateral government economic aid to the developing countries, both loans and grants, is basically a post-World-War-II phenomenon. Earlier loans, in both Africa and Latin America, seem to have been private arrangements, in many cases made by floating bonds in the international money market. This source became unavailable to Latin America when major defaults occurred during the 1930s and to Africa, especially after independence.

As was the case with foreign investment, most Latin American bilateral aid comes from the United States; in fact, approximately 90%, as Table 3 shows. The only other donors of any significance are Germany, which has provided almost 6% of net bilateral funds during the 1960s, and Canada, which has provided slightly over 2%. Major governmental aid to Latin America dates only to the early 1960s and the Alliance for Progress. Previously, the North American government had been almost entirely impervious to Latin American complaints that they were being ignored while Europe was the beneficiary of all the economic largesse through the Marshall Plan. Between 1945 and 1957, Latin America received only 2.5% of all U.S. aid; Yugoslavia, for example, received more U.S. assistance than all Latin American countries together (Block, 1968: 188). The United States seemed interested in Latin America only insofar as these countries backed its foreign policy interests, and thus it was only when Castro allied himself with the Soviet bloc that the United States began sending significant sums of government aid to the south. The amounts, as can be seen from Table 3, varied from year to year, but averaged somewhat less than $700 million annually.[14]

TABLE 3

Net Bilateral Aid by Major Donors, 1960-1967 (millions of U.S. dollars)[a]

Region	Belgium	Canada	France	Germany	Italy	Sino-Soviet	United Kingdom	United States	Totals Without Sino-Soviet	Totals With Sino-Soviet	% Increase or Decrease (without Sino-Soviet)
AFRICA											
1960	$ 86.0		$ 307.5	$ 5.3	$ 16.6	$ 90.0	$ 123.6	$ 39.0	$ 578.7	$ 668.7	
1961	70.5		304.0	13.4	18.5	310.0	228.0	75.0	710.8	1,020.8	22.8
1962	63.4		325.9	59.2	12.5	35.0	172.5	197.0	833.4	864.4	17.2
1963	75.8		337.3	54.1	22.5	66.0	163.5	159.0	816.3	882.3	–2.1
1964	76.5		345.6	41.4	16.4	212.0	211.3	161.0	863.7	1,075.7	5.8
1965	96.0		319.2	61.2	26.8	78.0	210.0	248.0	984.2	1,062.2	13.9
1966	59.7		327.0	95.8	22.9	46.0	191.6	276.0	1,008.1	1,054.1	9.7
1967	63.1		386.0	74.2	57.5	119.0	176.6	221.0	1,028.4	1,147.4	2.0
Total	$591.0		$2,652.5	$404.6	$193.7	$957.0	$1,477.0	$1,376.0	$6,823.6	$7,780.6	
Average	$ 73.8		$ 331.5	$ 50.5	$ 24.2	$119.6	$ 184.6	$ 172.0	$ 852.9	$ 972.5	9.9
Source as % of total bilateral aid	8.6%[c] (7.5%)[d]		38.8% (34.0%)	5.9% (5.2%)	2.8% (2.4%)	– (12.2%)	21.6% (18.9%)	20.1% (17.6%)	100.0%[b] –	– (100.0%)[b]	

TABLE 3 (Continued)

Region	Belgium	Canada	France	Germany	Italy	Sino-Soviet	United Kingdom	United States	Totals Without Sino-Soviet	Totals With Sino-Soviet	% Increase or Decrease (without Sino-Soviet)
LATIN AMERICA[e]											
1960		$ 4.8		$ 23.3				$ 184.0	$ 206.3		
1961		3.8		30.6				702.0	735.0		256.2
1962		20.7		37.6				578.0	673.1		–8.5
1963		34.9		36.4				560.0	649.5		–5.6
1964		33.8		6.2				452.0	490.3		–24.6
1965		6.2		45.4				613.5	720.8		47.0
1966		3.6		46.0				723.0	762.8		5.8
1967		3.4		57.2				604.0	676.4		–11.4
Total		$111.1		$282.7				$4,416.5	$4,914.2		
Average		$ 13.8		$ 35.3				$ 552.0	$ 614.2		37.0
Source as % of total bilateral aid		2.2%		5.7%				89.8%	100.0%		

SOURCE: Calculated from OECD, **Geographical Distribution of Financial Flow to Less-Developed Countries, 1960-64, 1965, 1966-67** (for OECD countries); UN, **International Flow of Long-Term Capital and Official Donations, 1960-62, 1961-65, 1962-66, 1964-68** (for Sino-Soviet countries).

a. See note 17 on definition of "net."
b. Percentages for major donors do not add to 100% because of minor donors.
c. Percentage without Sino-Soviet aid.
d. Percentage including Sino-Soviet aid.
e. Excludes Soviet aid to Cuba because of lack of data (the commonly used figure is $365 million per year).

TABLE 4
Net Multilateral Aid by Donors, 1960-1967 (millions of U.S. dollars)[a]

Region	World Bank Group	Interamerican Development Bank	African Development Bank	EEC	UN	Total	% Increase (or decrease)
AFRICA							
1960	$ 48.7			$ 3.2	$ 16.0	$ 67.9	
1961	51.9			15.0	39.9	106.7	57.1
1962	44.0			51.2	29.5	124.7	16.8
1963	8.3			58.5	36.0	102.8	–17.6
1964	24.3		$ –3.2	77.3	52.6	151.0	46.8
1965	60.5			97.3	34.4	193.2	27.9
1966	50.8		–28.0	101.7	50.3	174.9	–9.5
1967	74.9		–28.0	94.8	50.3	192.0	9.7
Total	$363.5		$–59.2	$499.0	$308.9	$1,113.2	
Average	$ 45.4		$ –7.4	$ 62.3	$ 38.6	$ 139.1	18.7
Source as % of total multilateral aid	32.6%		–5.3%	44.8%	27.7%	100.0%	
LATIN AMERICA							
1960	$ 66.6	$ –68.7			$ 12.7	$ 10.7	
1961	47.9	–109.5			11.9	–48.9	–82.1
1962	99.8	–55.8			25.0	69.0	70.8
1963	180.6	74.4			30.2	265.1	284.3
1964	169.5	103.0			37.0	309.5	16.7
1965	130.7	–15.5			35.5	150.7	–51.4
1966	155.1	8.3			41.8	205.1	36.1
1967	145.2	113.8			41.8	300.8	46.5
Total	$995.4	$ 50.0			$235.9	$1,262.0	
Average	$124.4	$ 6.2			$ 29.4	$ 157.7	45.8
Source as % of total multilateral aid	78.6%	3.9%			18.6%	100.0%	

SOURCE: Calculated from OECD, **Geographical Distribution of Financial Flow to Less-Developed Countries, 1960-64, 1965, 1966-67.**

a. See note 17 for definition of "net."

The situation in Africa is somewhat more complex, since a greater number of donor countries are involved. The African figures for Table 3 have been calculated both with and without data for the "Sino-Soviet" countries. This is because it is even more difficult to find data for aid donations by the communist countries than for the western group. The major problem is that most available data are in the form of "commitments" which are then disbursed at an unspecified rate over a number of years. In addition, it is almost impossible to disaggregate the communist countries' figures–thus, the designation "Sino-Soviet." Looking at Table 3 first without the communist aid, it can be seen that France is by far the largest donor nation (38.8% of total black African aid), followed by the United Kingdom (21.6%), and the United States (20.1%). Others providing large sums include Belgium (8.6%), Germany (5.9%), and Italy (2.8%). When the Soviet figures are added, their proportion becomes 12.3%, and all of the others, of course, decline slightly, so that the communist bloc together becomes the fourth largest donor. Unlike the vacillating Latin American figures, African bilateral aid has increased *fairly* steadily each year (averaging around 10%) when the communist aid is not considered. The erratic nature of the latter makes the totals including them somewhat erratic also.

The third component of capital flow is multilateral aid. Multilateral aid is also a recent phenomenon in international relations, even newer than governmental bilateral aid. Multilateral donations are seen by the developing countries as preferable to other varieties of aid and, in fact, they have themselves taken the initiative in forming some of the proliferating multinational funding agencies. Although multinational sources were supposed to be an improvement, both because they would not have the fluctuations of bilateral aid and because they would lessen traditional ties to various Western governments, Table 4 indicates that these benefits may not have come about–not yet, at least. It will be noticed, for instance, that the largest source of multilateral aid to Africa (44.8%) is the European Economic Community (EEC) which means that the former French and Belgian colonies are still getting funds from their former mother countries. Likewise, the largest multilateral donor in Latin America (78.6%) is the so-called World Bank Group, which is the source with the largest amount of control by the United States (which has the power, for example, to appoint the World Bank's president). Africa also gets a significant amount of its multilateral funds from the World Bank Group (32.6%). The other multilateral sources for both regions are the United Nations and the regional development banks. UN funds–probably the most truly "multinational" source–are more important for Africa than

TABLE 5
Aid Concentration, 1967 (percentage of total official bilateral flow coming from major donor country)

Recipient Country	% Without Sino-Soviet Aid	% Including Sino-Soviet Aid	Major Donor Country
AFRICA			
Burundi	79.4	79.4	Belgium
Cameroun	67.6	67.6	France
Central African Republic	92.6	90.6	France
Chad	68.2	68.2	France
Congo (Brazzaville)	78.5	51.6	France
Congo (Kinshasa)	51.7	51.7	Belgium
Dahomey	59.4	59.4	France
Ethiopia	52.4	36.0	United States
Gabon	70.0	70.0	France
Ghana	49.0	40.2	United States
Guinea	88.7	58.4	United States[a]
Ivory Coast	87.2	87.2	France
Kenya	64.1	54.0	United Kingdom
Liberia	95.6	95.6	United States
Malagasy Republic	90.2	90.2	France
Malawi	79.5	79.5	United Kingdom
Mali	75.4	49.2	France[a]
Mauritania	98.8	98.8	France
Niger	73.9	73.9	France
Nigeria	49.5	43.2	United States
Rwanda	64.8	64.8	Belgium
Senegal	85.0	83.4	France
Sierra Leone	60.7	43.8	United States
Somali Republic	54.2	45.5	United States[a]
Sudan	39.7	30.5	United States
Tanzania[b]	31.4	26.0	United Kingdom
Togo	49.1	49.1	Germany
Uganda	64.7	54.1	United Kingdom
Upper Volta	79.7	79.7	France
Zambia	58.7	57.0	United Kingdom
Median	67.9	58.9	
Range	31.4-98.8	26.0-98.8	

for Latin America (27.7% for the former versus 18.6% for the latter). The development banks in both regions are the least important source of multilateral funds. Africa's bank, which had not really gotten started in the period covered by these data, provided a negative net amount, while the Interamerican Development Bank provided less than 4% of Latin American funds.[15] Fluctuation in multilateral aid is more of a problem

TABLE 5 (Continued)

	Percentage	Donor Country
LATIN AMERICA		
Argentina	–[c]	–
Bolivia	93.9	United States
Brazil	122.3[e]	United States
Chile	61.0	United States
Colombia	94.8	United States
Costa Rica	96.0	United States
Cuba	–[d]	Sino-Soviet
Dominican Republic	99.6	United States
Ecuador	94.9	United States
El Salvador	96.2	United States
Guatemala	92.1	United States
Haiti	88.4	United States
Honduras	97.5	United States
Mexico	80.0	United States
Nicaragua	98.0	United States
Panama	110.5[e]	United States
Paraguay	42.9	United States
Peru	57.5	United States
Uruguay	91.4	United States
Venezuela	95.9	United States
Median	94.9	
Range	42.9-122.3	

SOURCE: Calculated from OECD, **Geographical Distribution of Financial Flow to Less-Developed Countries, 1966-67**; Kamarck (1971: 329) (see text for way in which Sino-Soviet aid was calculated).

a. Sino-Soviet countries become the major donor when they are added in.

b. Tanzanian percentages are based on an average over the period 1965-1967 because of significant fluctuations in donors from year to year. Although the United Kingdom appears as the largest donor by this method, it should be noted that U.K. aid was rapidly decreasing during the period to the extent that it was only the fourth largest donor in 1967.

c. Argentina has been left out since its net bilateral flow has been negative since 1964.

d. There are no accurate estimates of aid to Cuba, but 90% would probably be a good guess as to concentration.

e. Percentages are over 100% because outflow to certain countries made the U.S. contribution larger than the total **net** inflow.

in Latin America than in Africa, as can be seen by the percentage increase and decrease figures in Table 4.

Three questions remain concerning the comparison of capital flow in Africa and Latin America. The first involves the concentration of bilateral aid in individual countries. (The question should also be examined for foreign investment, but the data do not permit this.) That is, Table 3 shows that the African area *as a whole* has a greater variety of important donors than does Latin America, but it might be that the concentration *within* individual countries is quite similar in the two regions, with French aid going almost entirely to former French colonies, and so on. To find out if this is true, an index of aid concentration was constructed consisting of percentage of aid coming from the major donor for each country. Again, two sets of calculations are shown, one based on funds from OECD countries and the second including "Sino-Soviet" aid. Due to the problem of commitments and disbursements mentioned above, a rough estimate of disbursements for any given year was made by averaging commitments over a 10-year period and assuming that approximately one-tenth of that sum would have been disbursed in any one year. (Since the year involved is 1967–the end of the 10-year period–this assumption may not be too far off for that year.) As can be seen in Table 5, the spread of donors in the African region as a whole does seem to be replicated in the individual countries. That is, the concentration as measured by median figures is far higher in Latin America than in Africa–94.9% as opposed to 67.9% for OECD countries only, and 94.9% as opposed to 58.9% when "Sino-Soviet" countries are included.

A second question has to do with the relative importance of different

TABLE 6
Gross Inflow of Foreign Capital by Types, 1960-1967
(millions of U.S. dollars)[a]

	Total (1960-1967)	Average (1960-1967)	Type as % of Grand Total
AFRICA			
Private investment	2,248.9	281.1	23.5
Official Bilateral Aid			
Loans	1,870.2	233.8	19.5
Grants	4,378.8	547.3	45.7
Total	6,249.0	781.1	65.3
Multilateral aid	1,068.3	133.5	11.1
Grand total	9,566.2	1,195.7	100.1
LATIN AMERICA			
Private investment	6,293.3	786.7	46.4
Official Bilateral Aid			
Loans	4,505.1	563.1	33.2
Grants	1,488.7	186.1	11.0
Total	5,994.0	749.2	44.2
Multilateral aid	1,247.0	155.9	9.2
Grand total	13,534.3	1,691.8	100.0

SOURCE: Calculated from OECD, **Geographical Distribution of Financial Flow to Less-Developed Countries, 1960-64, 1965, 1966-67.**

a. See note 16 for definition of "gross" as used in this table.

types of foreign aid–private investment, bilateral grants, bilateral loans, and multilateral aid. Table 6 shows the figures for *gross* capital flow of each type.[16] Here it will be seen that the mix of the four types of capital is very different in the two regions. In Africa, the largest amount is from bilateral grants (45.7%), while this source accounts for only 11.0% of the capital flow in Latin America. The largest share in Latin America, on the other hand, is from private investment (46.4%), which provides only 23.5% of total funds in Africa. Bilateral loans are almost twice as important in Latin America–33.2% as opposed to only 19.5% in Africa–while multilateral aid (grants and loans) is least important in both regions–11.1% in Africa and 9.2% in Latin America.

The final question concerns the *net* flow of money to the African and Latin American countries. As indicated in note 16, there is a good deal of trouble figuring out net amounts (which, after all, is what concerns the recipient countries themselves), but I have made some rough estimates which again reveal vast differences between the two regions. The estimates were made as follows: (1) private investment–from the "gross" figures

TABLE 7
Net Inflow of Foreign Capital, 1960-1967
(millions of U.S. dollars)[a]

	Total (1960-1967)	Average (1960-1967)
AFRICA		
Gross inflow	9,566.2	1,195.7
Service Payments		
Amortization and interest	2,145.0	,268.1
Profits	3,598.2	449.7
Total	5,743.2	717.9
Net inflow	3,823.0	477.8
LATIN AMERICA		
Gross inflow	13,534.3	1,691.8
Service Payments		
Amortization and interest	5,004.3	625.5
Profits	12,778.0	1,597.2
Total	17,782.3	2,222.7
Net inflow	–4,248.0	–531.0

SOURCES: Gross inflow—from Table 6. Amortization and interest—data were obtained by multiplying gross bilateral and multilateral loans from Table 6 by service payment percentages, as given in Pearson et al. (1969: 74). See note 17 for further discussion. Profits—United Nations (1962-1966: 72) for 1960-1966 for Latin America. Data were corrected by subtracting out figures for Guyana, Jamaica, Surinam, and Trinidad/Tobago. Based on the 1960-1966 data, an estimate of $2,000 million was made for 1967; Kamarck (1971: 121) for 1963-1967 for Africa. To get profit data for 1960-1962, the average ratio of profits to investment for 1963-1967 was computed, and this ratio was multiplied by investment figures for 1960-1962.

a. See text and note 17 for details on computations.

TABLE 8

Destination of Exports, 1960-1966 (in percentages)

Region	North America			Western Europe				Japan	Sino-Soviet	Own Region	Rest of World
	U.S.	Canada	Total	EEC	EFTA	Other	Total				
AFRICA											
1960	9.8	0.4	(10.2)	44.2	22.1	0.7	(67.0)	1.5	5.7	6.8	8.7
1961	9.8	0.6	(10.4)	46.0	22.1	0.0	(68.1)	1.6	5.0	6.6	8.3
1962	8.3	0.5	(8.8)	47.7	20.7	1.9	(70.3)	1.4	6.0	6.5	7.0
1963	7.6	0.7	(8.3)	47.4	20.3	2.3	(70.0)	1.9	6.5	5.9	7.3
1964	8.4	0.7	(9.1)	45.7	18.9	3.2	(67.8)	2.3	5.8	7.6	7.4
1965	7.6	0.6	(8.2)	44.9	19.9	3.2	(68.0)	2.1	7.4	7.7	6.8
1966	7.7	0.9	(8.6)	46.0	18.5	3.0	(67.5)	2.5	6.7	7.6	7.2
Average (1960-1966)	8.4	0.7	(9.1)	46.0	20.4	2.0	(68.4)	1.9	6.1	6.9	6.8
LATIN AMERICA											
1960	41.8	1.7	(43.5)	18.4	11.7	1.5	(31.6)	2.8	3.1	7.9	11.1
1961	37.7	1.8	(39.5)	18.5	11.3	2.0	(31.8)	3.9	5.8	6.7	12.3
1962	36.0	3.1	(39.1)	20.0	10.9	2.0	(32.9)	3.7	5.4	7.2	11.8
1963	34.5	3.3	(37.8)	21.0	10.8	2.3	(34.1)	4.3	4.8	7.7	11.3
1964	32.2	2.9	(35.1)	20.8	10.2	2.7	(33.7)	4.7	5.0	9.2	12.3
1965	32.0	2.9	(34.9)	19.9	9.6	3.2	(32.7)	4.3	6.6	9.8	11.7
1966	33.2	2.5	(35.7)	19.7	9.1	3.5	(32.3)	4.7	6.4	9.8	11.1
Average (1960-1966)	35.3	2.6	(37.9)	19.7	10.5	2.5	(32.7)	4.1	5.3	8.3	11.6

SOURCES: ECLA, **Economic Survey, 1966:** 39 for Latin America; ECA, **Economic Bulletin, (1969), IX, 1 (June):** 21 for Africa.

TABLE 9

Origin of Imports, 1960-1966 (in percentages)

Region	North America			Western Europe							
	U.S.	Canada	Total	EEC	EFTA	Other	Total	Japan	Sino-Soviet	Own Region	Rest of World
AFRICA											
1960	7.2	0.4	(7.6)	47.1	19.5	1.6	(68.2)	4.7	4.4	5.7	9.4
1961	8.8	0.5	(9.3)	42.8	19.1	1.4	(63.3)	5.1	6.0	5.5	10.7
1962	12.1	0.5	(12.6)	39.4	18.8	1.5	(59.7)	4.4	6.2	5.8	11.3
1963	10.5	0.5	(11.0)	39.8	19.1	1.9	(60.8)	5.9	7.0	5.6	9.7
1964	11.4	0.5	(11.9)	36.5	17.9	1.5	(55.9)	6.6	6.8	7.4	11.4
1965	9.4	0.5	(9.9)	36.1	17.5	1.7	(55.3)	8.2	8.3	7.4	10.8
1966	11.2	0.4	(11.6)	35.3	16.8	2.1	(54.2)	7.3	7.8	7.6	11.2
Average (1960-1966)	10.0	0.5	(10.5)	39.6	18.4	1.7	(59.6)	6.0	6.6	6.4	10.6
LATIN AMERICA											
1960	44.0	2.5	(46.5)	20.1	11.5	1.6	(33.2)	3.5	2.9	8.7	5.2
1961	41.1	2.8	(43.9)	21.1	11.1	1.6	(33.8)	3.9	7.5	7.1	3.8
1962	39.0	2.6	(41.6)	20.2	10.6	1.8	(32.6)	3.9	8.5	8.1	5.3
1963	39.3	3.1	(42.4)	18.8	10.0	1.6	(30.4)	4.0	9.3	9.4	4.5
1964	41.4	3.4	(44.8)	17.5	9.1	1.9	(28.5)	4.4	7.7	10.6	4.0
1965	40.0	3.2	(43.2)	17.5	9.3	2.1	(28.9)	4.4	7.7	11.6	4.2
1966	40.3	3.3	(43.6)	17.7	9.2	2.7	(29.6)	4.5	7.6	11.0	3.7
Average (1960-1966)	40.7	2.9	(43.6)	18.9	10.1	1.9	(30.9)	4.1	7.3	9.5	4.4

SOURCES: ECA, **Economic Bulletin, (1969) IX, 1 (June):** 24 for Africa; ECLA, **Economic Survey, 1967:** 141 for Latin America.

shown in Table 6 was subtracted the amount of profits which went back to the home country; (2) grants were left as is; (3) bilateral and multilateral loans–from the "gross" amounts shown in Table 6 was subtracted the amortization and interest paid. The data for the latter come from the Pearson Commission (Pearson et al., 1969: 76), which estimates that, for the period 1965-1967, Africa spent 73% of gross loans as debt service and Latin America spent 87%. (By 1977, they conclude, if the gross flow remains constant, Africa will be paying 121% and Latin America, 130%).[17]

After making these adjustments, the following conclusion emerges: Latin America has actually provided a net *outflow* of foreign capital amounting to about $500 million a year over the eight-year period examined here, while Africa seems to have profited from a net *inflow* of almost $500 million per year. Some of the implications of these observations will be discussed in the concluding section of the paper.

TRADE

A second aspect of economic dependency involves trade relations. That is, the larger the percentage of its exports a country sends to any one other country–the greater its economic dependency. As a means of providing foreign exchange, and therefore increasing a country's capacity to import needed goods, exports are far more important than foreign capital inflow. During the 1960s, exports were over four times as important as all gross foreign capital combined (loans, grants, private investment) in Africa, and seven times as important in Latin America (calculated from balance of payments data in Kamarck, 1971: 121; Whitehead, 1971: 216).

Tables 8 and 9 show the destination of African and Latin American exports and the origins of their imports, respectively. As might be expected, the countries important in trade relations are the same ones that were important with respect to capital flow. For the black African countries as a whole, the concentration on Western Europe for trade partners is of about the same magnitude as aid concentration (around 68%), whereas Latin America's trade partners are far more dispersed than its aid donors (compare Tables 3 and 8). Only 35% of its exports from 1960-1966 went to the United States when, by comparison, almost 90% of its bilateral aid came from there. Western Europe has been slightly more important to Africa as a provider of imports than as a receiver of exports but, in general, the percentage of exports from and imports to any one country or area is fairly similar.

The trend data for the two regions from 1960 to 1966 do not show any major changes. The African export percentages show the United States and the European Free Trade Association (EFTA) group becoming *slightly* less important while Japan, Africa itself, and the Sino-Soviet countries have become slightly more important. Import trends for Africa again show the latter three areas plus the United States slightly more important, while both the EFTA and EEC groups become less significant. Latin American trade trends between 1960 and 1966 show their major trading partner, the United States, becoming somewhat less dominant for both exports and imports, and Europe becoming less important for the latter and about the same for the former. As with Africa, trade with Japan, its own region, and the Sino-Soviet group seem to have increased somewhat though not dramatically. (The increased trade between the Sino-Soviet countries and Latin America is mainly due to increased trade with Cuba, although Mexico has also increased its trade with them; U.S. Agency for International Development, 1967).

Export data going back to the 1950s show the same general trends as do the data for the 1960s, with the most conspicuous fact again being the very *lack* of change. Thus, for instance, African trade showed no major differences before and after independence.[18]

As was the case with bilateral aid, it is necessary to look at individual African and Latin American countries to see how they fare on trade concentration, since regional totals may not be representative of the situation in individual countries. Table 10 shows the major receiver and the percentage of exports going to that country in 1967 for each African and Latin American country. The median and range show that, unlike the aid situation, there is not much difference in trade concentration between the two regions, although Latin America has a slightly higher median—37.2% compared with 34.1% for Africa. The United States is the major export receiver for 15 of the 19 Latin American countries for which data were available. The exceptions were Argentina (Italy as its major receiver), Cuba (USSR), Nicaragua (Japan), and Uruguay (United Kingdom). In Africa, the vast majority of countries kept their former mother countries as their major trading partners into the postcolonial period. Exceptions were Congo-Brazzaville (Netherlands), Ghana (United States), Mali (Senegal), Nigeria (United States), Somalia (Arabia), and the Sudan (Germany). Ethiopia also had the United States as its major export receiver.

Traditional trading ties may also be reinforced (or regulated) through the use of tariffs, quotas, and preferential access to markets. With one exception to be mentioned below, "positive" use of tariffs, quotas, and

TABLE 10
Trade Concentration, 1967 (percentage of exports going to most important trading partner)

Country	Percentage	Partner
AFRICA		
Burundi	–	–
Cameroun	33.7	France
Central African Republic	42.0	France
Chad	56.8	France
Congo (Brazzaville)	20.5	Netherlands
Congo (Kinshasa)	29.9	Belgium
Dahomey	34.6	France
Ethiopia	43.1	United States
Gabon	35.5	France
Ghana	20.7	United States
Guinea	–	–
Ivory Coast	37.3	France
Kenya	24.0	United Kingdom
Liberia	29.9	United States
Malagasy Republic	36.6	France
Malawi	55.0	United Kingdom
Mali	32.0	Senegal
Mauritania	20.6	France
Niger	76.4	France
Nigeria	29.5	United States
Rwanda	31.1	Belgium
Senegal	66.2	France
Sierra Leone	70.3	United Kingdom
Somali Republic	56.2	Arabia
Sudan	11.8	Germany
Tanzania	30.0	United Kingdom
Togo	37.9	France
Uganda	23.7	United Kingdom
Upper Volta	49.3	France
Zambia	27.3	United Kingdom
Median	34.1	
Range	11.8-70.3	
LATIN AMERICA		
Argentina	15.6	Italy
Bolivia	43.4	United States
Brazil	33.1	United States
Chile	18.4	United States
Colombia	43.5	United States
Costa Rica	47.7	United States
Cuba	46.2	USSR
Dominican Republic	86.9	United States
Ecuador	48.7	United States
El Salvador	22.9	United States
Guatemala	31.2	United States
Haiti	–	–
Honduras	45.9	United States
Mexico	54.5	United States
Nicaragua	31.1	Japan
Panama	76.8	United States
Paraguay	25.1	United States
Peru	37.2	United States
Uruguay	21.5	United Kingdom
Venezuela	42.8[a]	United States
Median	37.2	
Range	15.6-86.9	

SOURCE: United Nations (1968).

a. Total export value excludes Netherlands Antilles since this is almost never an ultimate destination.

preferences has been much more common in the African countries than in Latin America. During the colonial period, the French colonies enjoyed not only preferential access to the French market for their primary products but, in addition, they received price guarantees which were often above the world market prices. In return, the colonies largely reserved their markets for French goods. Britain has also allowed duty-free entry to products of Commonwealth countries, though few preferences are given in return. During the 1960s, the system changed for former French, Belgian, and Italian colonies as the EEC apparatus went into effect. (Presumably, the former British colonies will now also come under a new agreement which is supposed to be negotiated by 1975.) Under the Yaounde Convention, first signed in 1964, a preferential trade zone was established between the EEC and the Associated States in Africa. This agreement provided for the Associated States to receive duty-free entry for many of their products, and, in addition, these products were to be protected from competition by tariffs on goods from other producers. (Products which are competitive with those grown in the EEC itself are not so well treated.) Although they acquired duty-free entrance to the entire Common Market area instead of just to France, with the establishment of the EEC, former French colonies nevertheless suffered because they lost their price supports which were very important for many products—especially peanuts, but also sugar, cotton, coffee, palm oil, and the like. To offset this loss in export revenue, the EEC set up the Fund for Economic Development to provide financial aid to African countries (see Table 4). In addition to the former French, Belgian, and Italian colonies, several former British colonies have already negotiated special arrangements with the EEC. Nigeria, Tanzania, Kenya, and Uganda have acquired quotas and duty-free entry for many of their products, in return for which they give tariff preferences to EEC products and permit private corporations from EEC countries to establish in their countries (for the discussion on trade, see Kamarck, 1971: 82-110).

The United States has traditionally been less "generous" toward Latin America than Europe has been with Africa insofar as trade is concerned. The only major preferential system in the inter-American system was the Cuban sugar quota, whereby a certain amount of the U.S. market was reserved for Cuban sugar at prices generally higher than the world market. The effect was that almost all Cuban sugar was sold in the United States. This agreement, as will be remembered, was the major economic leverage with which the United States tried to influence the Castro government and, because of the lack of diversified market it represented, was one of the major reasons the Cubans became so dependent on the Soviet Union.

Otherwise, quotas and tariffs have generally been used to limit the entry of Latin American products into the U.S. market rather than to aid Latin American exports. (Even the sugar quota was long fought by U.S. sugar producers.) Major examples include the quotas on Venezuelan oil, as well as more general restrictions on textiles and manufactured goods.

The most recent development with respect to preferences is the work of the United Nations Conference on Trade and Development (UNCTAD). UNCTAD is interested in establishing a system whereby all developed countries would eliminate duties on manufactured products from all underdeveloped countries while maintaining them on imports from other developed countries. While the Africans do not object to this plan, it would not be of as direct advantage to them as it would be to Latin American countries, which are more industrialized. Such a system is very

TABLE 11
Export Commodity Concentration, 1967 (three leading exports as percentage of total exports)

Africa	%	Latin America	%
Burundi	92	Argentina	57
Cameroun	69	Bolivia	74
Central African Republic	90	Brazil	54
Chad	93	Chile	75
Congo (Brazzaville)	82	Colombia	83
Congo (Kinshasa)	71	Costa Rica	66
Dahomey	38	Cuba	93
Ethiopia	77	Dominican Republic	72
Gabon	82	Ecuador	86
Ghana	79	El Salvador	58
Guinea	81	Guatemala	56
Ivory Coast	75	Haiti	68
Kenya	58	Honduras	69
Liberia	96	Mexico	26
Malagasy Republic	51	Nicaragua	69
Malawi	74	Panama	88
Mali	69	Paraguay	58
Mauritania	97	Peru	55
Niger	86	Uruguay	67
Nigeria	71	Venezuela	96
Rwanda	92	Median	68
Senegal	78	Range	26-96
Sierra Leone	88		
Somali Republic	87		
Sudan	75		
Tanzania	45		
Togo	79		
Uganda	87		
Upper Volta	83		
Zambia	97		
Median	80		
Range	38-97		

SOURCE: Kamarck (1971: 112-114) for Africa; United Nations (1968) for Latin America.

important to the major Latin American countries–especially Brazil, Mexico, and Argentina–which are now reaching the end of the import substitution process in their own markets and are prevented by quotas or tariffs from competing in the developed countries (or even other underdeveloped countries). As Kamarck (1971: 108) suggests, however, industrial preferences might help Africa by encouraging industrialization and by helping Latin America expand its industrial exports and so enable the African countries to take over more of the primary product market.

One final item which is indirectly related to economic dependency is the tendency for Third World countries to rely on a few (nearly always primary) products as exports. Primary products are subject to sharp price fluctuations, and this concentration increases the problem, since a price drop for one or two commodities can reduce government revenue by large amounts. This is especially true for Burundi, Chad, Liberia, Mauritania, Senegal, and Zambia in Africa, and Venezuela and Cuba in Latin America, each of which receives at least 75% of its export revenue from a single product. This tends to make Third World countries more tied than they otherwise might be to guaranteed markets and prices. In addition, loss of export money due to fluctuations makes various kinds of foreign assistance more necessary. Table 11 shows the percentage of African and Latin American exports made up by the three leading export commodities. As can be seen, the median concentration is somewhat higher in Africa (80%) than in Latin America (68%).

FOREIGN MANPOWER

A third aspect of economic dependency involves the employment of foreign personnel and, to a lesser degree, foreign training of local students. Some parts of this topic tend to shade off into what might better be called cultural dependency, but there are important economic elements involved too.

There are a number of channels through which foreign manpower is provided to less-developed countries–bilateral technical assistance; multilateral technical assistance; foreign investment; other private groups such as foundations, churches, and the like; and contractual consultant services, among others. Only the first three types will be discussed here. Expatriates living in the less-developed countries are a somewhat different problem, but highly important in the African setting.

The patterns in the flow of foreign personnel are quite similar to those in foreign capital flow. That is, most of Africa's foreign manpower comes through bilateral (and, to a lesser extent, multilateral) technical assistance, while the majority of Latin American foreign manpower is provided through private investment. In addition, the proportions supplied by 'the various donor countries are similar: In Africa, 44% of technical assistance personnel come from France, 33% from the United Kingdom, 11% from the United States, 9% from Belgium, and some from the communist countries. In Latin America, practically all foreign manpower is provided by the United States (Maddison, 1965: 17, 21).

Table 12 gives data for bilateral technical assistance from OECD countries and shows the greater importance to Africa, in terms of number of persons involved as well as percentage of total aid devoted to technical assistance. Thirty-eight percent of total bilateral aid to Africa goes for technical assistance, while only 24% is involved in Latin America. Likewise, there are over 38,000 people involved in the program in Africa and less than 10,000 in Latin America.

Manpower assistance from the communist countries has generally been tied to specific projects. Thus, when they agree to finance a project, they will also provide the technicians necessary to carry it out. It is estimated that there were about 4,000 Soviet technicians in Africa in 1966, mostly located in Guinea, Mali, Ghana, Somalia, the Sudan, and Ethiopia. Cuba, of course, is the only Latin American country with any significant number of Soviet personnel. In addition to project aid, the Soviet Union provides manpower for industry, teaching, and medical work (Kamarck, 1971: 258; Maddison, 1965: 27-29). Chinese aid has gone mainly to three of the same countries–Guinea, Mali, and Somalia–and, in addition, to Tanzania and Kenya. Their best-known project is the Tan-Zam railroad, which will link the Zambian copper belt with the port of Dar es Salaam and thus lessen Zambian dependence on Rhodesia. One observer suggests that the fact that China is also a poor country makes its aid more useful in many ways to developing countries. For instance, the Chinese make fewer demands in the way of accommodations, they seem willing to work

TABLE 12
Bilateral Technical Assistance, 1965

	Africa	Latin America
Disbursements		
Technical assistance (millions of dollars)	384.9	201.8
Technical assistance as % of total bilateral aid	38.3	24.1
Number of Personnel		
Teachers	15,211	2,124
Total bilateral	38,204	9,679

SOURCE: OECD (1968: 46).

harder, and they often provide technology which is more labor intensive than that of the Soviet Union and the Western countries and, therefore, more adapted to the needs of developing countries (Maddison, 1965: 29).

Multilateral technical assistance has generally averaged about 15% of bilateral technical assistance (OECD, 1968: 44), but there seems to be no breakdown as to how it is distributed geographically, so no comparisons can be made here.

As with private investment in general, information on technical assistance provided through private investment is very hard to come by. One estimate (Maddison, 1965: 33) indicates there may have been around 35,000 American technicians, managers, and professional personnel, and twice that many Europeans, in the developing countries in the mid 1960s. Assuming that, since about two-thirds of U.S. investment in developing countries was in Latin America, about the same proportion of its manpower would be there; that would make about 24,000 people connected with private investment compared with less than 10,000 via technical assistance. (The latter figure does not include technical assistance in Cuba.) Using similar logic for the African case would suggest that perhaps 10,000 foreign personnel, American and European, would be provided through foreign investment channels, compared to almost 40,000 via technical assistance.[19]

Another aspect of the foreign manpower situation is students sent abroad to be trained. As can be seen in Table 13, this form of technical assistance is *relatively* more important in Latin America than in Africa. That is, there were less than one-half as many scholarships given out as experts financed in Africa, while there were one and a half times as many scholarships as experts in Latin America. In *absolute* terms, however, there were less than one-half as many scholarships given out in Latin America as in Africa. Table 13 also gives some indication of the percentage of university students studying abroad as opposed to at home. Here we see that study abroad is about ten times as important in Africa as in Latin

TABLE 13
Importance of Foreign Training, 1963

	Africa	Latin America
Scholarships	13,756	6,993
Experts	31,262	4,609
Ratio of scholarships to experts	.4	1.5
% of university students studying abroad	35.8[a]	2.1

SOURCE: Calculated from Maddison (1965: Tables, 2, 3, 5 and I-4).

a. Based on data for only eight countries—Congo (Kinshasa), Gabon, Ghana, Kenya, Madagascar, Nigeria, Sudan, Tanzania.

America. (Since these data are for the early 1960s, the situation in Africa may have changed somewhat as more universities have been founded or enlarged.)

In connection with foreign training, one final item must be added which is somewhat analogous to profits on foreign investment or interest on foreign loans. In other words, it is important to get some idea of the importance of the "brain drain" in taking trained (usually foreign trained) personnel *out* of Africa and Latin America. Once again, the data are sketchy at best. A report recently published by the Committee on International Migration of Talent (Education and World Affairs, 1970: 19-29) discussed the migration of persons with "highly developed professional and technical skills"–journalists, lawyers, civil servants, bankers, business executives, military officers, scientists, engineers, and physicians–from underdeveloped to developed countries. They estimate that this group averaged about 50,000 per year during the 1960s (about one-sixth of the total migration of workers from less-developed to developed countries). Of these 50,000, they say that almost all were from Cuba, southern Europe and Asia, with only about 3,000 per year coming from the rest of Latin America and 1,000 per year from Africa. On the other hand, migration from Latin America has gone down during the late 1960s, whereas it has gone up for Africa, as can be seen in Table 14.

Although the committee says that the brain drain problem is more important in Latin America than in Africa, it actually is the other way around, if seen in relative rather than absolute terms. Because Africa has far fewer professional personnel than Latin America, the loss is more significant. An example can be seen by looking at the number of physicians in the two regions–there are about 8,000 doctors in Africa and 130,000 in Latin America.[20] If we were to assume that ten percent of the professional migrants were doctors, that would mean around 100 doctors left Africa annually and 300 left Latin America. But 100 is 1.2%

TABLE 14
Index of Immigration of Professional and Technical Workers into the United States, 1964-1969

Year	Africa	Latin America
1964	100	100
1965	80	85
1966	120	70
1967	165	60
1968	240	70
1969	375	65

NOTE: Base year is 1964.
SOURCE: Estimates from graph in Education and World Affairs (1970: 28).

TABLE 15
Personnel (excluding teachers) Supplied by OECD Bilateral Technical Assistance, 1963

	Africa		Latin America	
	n	%	n	%
Education	424	2.0	225	13.0
Public administration	7,518	36.6	301	17.4
Agriculture	3,384	16.5	282	16.3
Industry	4,003	19.5	314	18.2
Health and sanitation	1,857	9.0	178	10.3
Other	3,312	16.1	423	24.5
Total	20,498	100.0	1,723	100.0

SOURCE: Maddison (1965: Table I-12).

of all African doctors and 300 is only 0.2% of Latin American doctors. The same probably holds for other professions as well.

Before finishing the discussion on foreign manpower, it is necessary to at least mention the problem of settlers in Africa. Shortly before independence in East Africa, it was estimated that Africans were only 6% of high-level manpower in Kenya, 13% in Tanganyika, and 16% in Uganda (Hunter. 1963). The figures were probably higher for British colonies in West Africa and lower for those of France and Belgium. Since a large number of non-Africans left after independence and the pressures for "Africanization," especially of the civil service, forced leaders to fire others, a personnel crisis ensued. The resulting situation can perhaps best be seen by looking back to the discussion, where it was pointed out that the majority of all positions in Africa demanding high-level skills are filled by foreigners provided by technical assistance or foreign investment. In addition, Table 15 shows the distribution of OECD personnel in Africa and Latin America. The extensive use of foreigners in public administration positions, usually the first to be filled by nationals, is another indication of the vast manpower gaps in Africa even compared to the Third World.

CONCLUSIONS

Before a discussion of some implications of the data just presented, it might be helpful to give a brief summary. Three basic points are especially important:

(1) Economic capacity: The section on economic overview shows that, in terms of traditional indicators (GNP, industrialization, infra-

structure, educational level, and so on), Latin America is definitely more "developed" than Africa; that is, its economic capacity is greater and is growing at a more rapid rate.

(2) Economic equality: The overview section also shows (although less clearly) that Latin American nations are in general more highly stratified, that there are more interest groups desirous of preserving or enlarging their privileges, and that there is thus a greater degree of inequality in Latin America than in Africa.

(3) Economic dependency: Two somewhat contradictory trends appear in the data on foreign capital, trade, and manpower. On the one hand, Africa is much more reliant on foreign assistance than is Latin America. A larger percentage of its gross investment comes from foreign capital; a larger percentage of its GDP derives from foreign trade; and a larger percentage of its manpower is of foreign origin. On the other hand, African nations are *less* dependent on any *one* advanced country than are the Latin American nations. The sources of their foreign capital, trade and manpower are more diversified among the advanced countries, while Latin America is primarily reliant on one country (the United States) for all of the above. Thus, in terms of the operational definition of dependency used in this study, involving *concentration* of foreign assistance with the concomitant possibilities of influence by the advanced countries, Latin America is more dependent than Africa.

It is precisely this "package"–increasing economic capacity in the aggregate sense although purchased at the cost of dependency and inequality–that has been called "dependent development" (for discussions of the concept of dependent development, see the citations in note 1). We will return to a discussion of this concept below. The dilemma for Latin America, of course, is how to maintain, or preferably accelerate, economic growth while eliminating the dependency and inequality that have traditionally accompanied it. For Africa, the problem is similar–how to achieve economic growth without increasing dependency and inequality. It is in this respect that there may be certain "lessons" which Latin America can offer African and other Third World countries.

(1) Foreign capital: The Latin American experience tends to indicate that the biggest problems with foreign capital come when a large portion of it is in the form of private investment. This type of capital comes to the Third World for the purpose of making profits as defined by the firm; the effect of the investment on the "host" country is secondary or irrelevant. In general, this effect is negative for at least three reasons:

(1) Drain of capital: If the data on direct investment in Table 6 are compared with those for profits in Table 7, it is apparent that both

Africa and Latin America had an outflow of capital with respect to private investment during the period studied. Latin American data for the 1950s show the same relationship for that decade (see Furtado, 1970: 168-169).[21] The comparison between "new" investment and profits does not really tell the whole story, however, since almost 60% of "new" investment is really reinvestment and another large chunk (about 25%) comes from loans to foreign corporations from Latin American banks (UN Economic Commission for Latin America, 1970: 313). (It is usually easier for foreigners to get loans than for nationals.)[22]

(2) Size: A second, and equally serious, problem stems from the size of many of the companies doing the investing. Data for Latin America show that many of the multinational corporations operating there have gross revenues larger than those of the countries themselves (McCamant, 1971: 22); this, of course, would be even more true for Africa. Therefore, not only do local companies, whether state-owned or private, have trouble competing with these giants, but governments have trouble regulating them. Since foreign corporations are often given special privileges to induce them to come, this further decreases the possibility of competition.

(3) Foreign government interference: Finally, there is the fact that a large amount of accumulated investment by its nationals tends to make a foreign government more likely to take steps to protect that investment. There are many examples in Latin America of the United States taking action ranging from cutting off aid to sending in troops, at least in part to protect U.S. private investment. A recent case is the refusal of the Export-Import Bank to lend money to Chile to buy airplanes. According to the *New York Times* for August 14, 1972, State Department officials say that the decision was made at the White House level under pressure from private North American companies. This decision was later expanded by Nixon's announcement that bilateral aid will be cut off, and support will be withheld from multilateral aid, for any country which has nationalized U.S. property without "prompt and just compensation" (*New York Times,* January 20, 1972).[23] In other words, it is difficult to view U.S. bilateral aid separately from private investment.[24]

This linkage was carried further since, in the past, almost all U.S. aid came in the form of "tied" credits (North American Congress for Latin America, 1972: 123). That is, aid funds had to be used to buy goods and services in the United States, even if they would be cheaper elsewhere. According to a recent UNCTAD (1967) study, because of the tied provision, Chilean costs for buying goods, for instance, were 12.5% above what they need have been.

(2) Foreign trade: For over twenty years now, Latin American

economists have been discussing the problems of heavy reliance on trade. Starting in 1949, the UN Economic Commission for Latin America (ECLA) began warning against building an export sector (usually one or two primary products) and using the foreign exchange earned thereby to import industrial goods and other needed items.[25] There were two basic arguments involved–first was the large price fluctuations for primary products which, in turn, affect government revenue, making any kind of long-term development planning almost impossible. The second argument was a more controversial one; it concerned what was called the deteriorating terms of trade for the Latin American countries. In essence, this argument said that the peripheral countries (Third World) were at a continual disadvantage vis-à-vis the center (industrialized nations) because the secular price trend for industrial goods was increasing while, for primary products, it was static or decreasing. Thus, the same quantity of primary products would finance fewer and fewer industrial goods (for critiques of the so-called ECLA doctrine, see Powelson, 1964: 294-296; Hirschman, 1961: 27-28, 37-42). ECLA's proposed solution for the Latin American countries was industrialization via import substitution in order to decrease dependency on external sources of supply. Unfortunately, however, the Latin American experience has hitherto been that import substitution has actually increased dependency because, instead of importing a variety of consumer and intermediate goods, imports now consist of raw materials and capital goods. Thus, when a restriction of imports becomes necessary, it causes a lowered growth rate and increased unemployment. Because of the small size of the internal market in most Latin American countries, industries operate at less than capacity, and therefore costs are high and tariff protection is necessary. This drives up prices to consumers. Selling on the international market is rarely possible, both because of higher prices for Third World products and because of tariffs and quotas (for more detailed discussions of import substitution, see Hirschman, 1969; Lessa, 1969). Although it was thought for a time that a Latin American common market would provide a solution to the above dilemma, this has so far failed both because countries were not willing to cooperate and because it became clear that the main group which would take advantage of the tariff revisions would be the multilateral corporations (Grunwald et al., 1971). The major lesson that Latin America has to offer here is that import substitution is not the panacea it was once thought to be.

(3) Foreign manpower: In recent years, Latin America has not had a large number of foreign personnel nor a large number of foreign-trained

local personnel. Those few that there have been, however, have been in key positions—managers of large corporations, top military officers, university professors, government advisers. Perhaps their most important effect has been a subtle one involving the importation of ideas, specifically the idea that the Third World countries should maintain the same kind of "standards" as the industrialized nations. One example concerns the type of technology to be employed. Since the Third World countries have a large supply of labor in relation to capital, it would seem to make sense to use some kind of labor-intensive rather than capital-intensive methods. The initiative here, however, would have to be taken by the Latin Americans themselves, since the multinational corporations have no incentive to apply such strategies. They (as opposed to the "host" countries) have access to plenty of capital (see Lessa, 1969: 52-90). A second problem concerns the types of products to be manufactured. As Ivan Illich (1969) says, what the Third World needs is not a luxury automobile which will go 70 mph on the highways and turn obsolete in three years but a "mechanical donkey" which is cheap, has no frills, will operate in all kinds of terrain, and will last at least a generation. Such products will not appear as long as the Third World relies on the advanced countries. A third example focuses on human rather than physical capital and involves the emphasis on what one observer (Helleiner, 1971: 102) calls "degree holders" at the expense of skilled workers. As he puts it, the opportunity costs of doctors and modern hospitals, for instance, are very high—50 rural dispensaries for one urban hospital, 100 medical assistants or midwives for one doctor. This is especially important in Africa, where over 90% of the people live in rural areas. A more general formulation of this problem involves a discussion of technological transfer—whether the Third World should establish its own research and development or merely rely on the advanced countries for technology (for discussions of current problems of science and technology in Latin America, see Herrera et al., 1970; Sunkel, 1970). In sum, it might be said that foreign and foreign-trained manpower may well have helped prevent Latin America from taking stock of its own situation and deciding what is necessary within the Latin American context rather than merely adopting U.S. methods.

These, then, have been three of the main external causes of dependent development. Let us now turn to the effect of dependent development as seen in Latin America. The main effect has been to promote economic growth at the same time that inequality was intensified. This double-edged result is inherent in the approach implied in dependent development: the basic idea is to build on the modern sector, assuming that the advantages will eventually "trickle down" to the lower classes. The trickling down has yet to occur in Latin America; in fact, just the opposite has happened.

The situation can best be seen by looking at Brazil and Mexico, the countries which have enjoyed the most rapid economic growth. In Brazil, which has grown at a rate of about 9% per year since 1967, the distribution among income groups became more unequal between 1960 and 1970. According to census figures, the top 3.2% of the population had about 27% of the income in 1960 compared with over 33% in 1970. Gini indices for the two years were .59 and .63 respectively (Fishlow, 1971: esp. Tables 1 and 5). Although Brazilian data are complicated by the attempt to halt inflation and the short time period involved, Mexico has experienced rapid economic growth since the 1940s without an inflation problem. The distribution trend, however, is quite similar. Mexican data for 1950, 1957, and 1963 show the lowest 40% of the population with an ever smaller share of the national income–14.3%, 11.3%, and 10.5% respectively. By some calculations, the top 5% has had a decreasing share, but by others, the share may well have been increasing.[26]

In addition to class inequality, regional inequality is also important. Traditionally, urban areas have been advantaged as compared to rural areas, and the capital city and its environs have been especially favored in terms of income and investment. For example, data for Mexico, Venezuela, and Brazil show that average income in the most favored regions is from 2.2 to 2.8 times that in the poorest areas (UN Economic Commission for Latin America, 1969: 402). The most significant point, however, is that this type of inequality has also been increasing under dependent development. In Mexico, the federal district has increased its dominance as compared to other regions of the country (Wilkie, 1967: 236-237, 248-249). The Brazilian Northeast has gotten poorer as São Paulo, the main industrial city of Brazil, has gotten richer.[27]

It is through this increasing inequality, both in terms of classes and of regions, that we can see how dependent development operates; that is, we can see the links between economic growth, on the one hand, and inequality and dependence on the other. Through building on the modern sector within the underdeveloped countries, aggregate figures such as GDP do increase. In a more primitive (enclave) economy, building on the modern sector has primarily meant investment in the export sector, which is directed toward the outside world and has very few links to the internal economy. In a more advanced economic setting (one characterized by a relatively large amount of import substituting industrialization), the situation is more complicated. There are linkages of various kinds between foreign corporations and the internal economy because industry requires markets as well as primary and intermediate inputs and skilled labor.[28]

The important point, however, is that these linkages tend to be concentrated among a relatively small percentage of the population, on both the production and the consumption sides. The interests of such groups, in turn, become more closely tied to those of the foreigners than to those of the rest of the national population. Such groups may include the industrial bourgeoisie, which needs capital, patents, and technology from abroad; the military, which is trained and equipped in the advanced countries; the workers in foreign plants, who form an "aristocracy of labor"; and certain middle sector groups, such as intellectuals, which find their reference groups in the industrialized nations. These domestic groups clearly have a vested interest in maintaining the system of dependency because they—together with their foreign allies—are the beneficiaries.[29]

The question becomes whether the benefits now monopolized by the few will indeed "trickle down" to the lower classes. As pointed out above, such has not been the case in Latin America. Furthermore, there is good reason to believe that the groups having control of economic resources, both the foreigners and their domestic allies, only become stronger with increasing economic growth and thus significant redistribution becomes ever *less* likely. There may be some redistribution from the upper class to the upper-middle class, but since the lower class is so large, not even the degree of equality which exists in the United States and Western Europe will result. In the latter countries, the bottom 20% of the population has an even lower percentage of the income than in many Latin American countries, but the remaining 80% is more evenly divided (UN Economic Commission for Latin America, 1969: 364-373).

What does all this imply about strategies for the future? Latin American and African alternatives may not be the same. Two things must be kept in mind: (1) Africa is currently far more in need of foreign assistance than is Latin America. The lower GNP means that there is lower gross savings, and therefore a smaller amount of domestic capital available. The small size of the population and the lack of industry indicates a heavy reliance on trade. The lack of infrastructure both indicates the need for more investment and prevents more rapid growth from taking place. The low level of literacy and the small number of university graduates narrows the pool from which personnel can be recruited. Finally, all these factors are not likely to change rapidly, since the rate of growth is lower than in either Latin America or the industrialized countries. (2) Africa is currently getting its aid on more favorable terms than Latin America. A much larger percentage of external capital flow in Africa is in the form of grants and, correspondingly, a much smaller percentage comes through foreign private investment, which represents a negative flow in both regions. In addition, more of the loans in Africa are on "soft" terms than is the case in Latin

TABLE 16
Public Debt Service and Investment Income Payment as Percentage of Exports, 1967 or 1968

Above 25%	20-25%	15-20%	10-15%	Below 10%
Latin America				
Brazil		Peru	Honduras	El Salvador
Mexico		Guatemala	Paraguay	
Argentina		Dominican Republic		
Colombia		Bolivia		
Venezuela		Uruguay		
Chile		Nicaragua		
		Costa Rica		
Africa				
		Nigeria	Ethiopia	Sudan
		Kenya	Uganda	Tanzania
		Malawi	Ivory Coast	
		Zambia		

SOURCE: Pearson et al. (1969: 374).

America. All this can be summed up by looking at debt statistics for the two regions. Table 16 shows profit outflow, interest and amortization as a percentage of exports for 25 African and Latin American nations.

In other words, even from a conventional economic viewpoint, the arguments for ending economic dependency in Latin America are strongly persuasive. If the data in Table 7 are correct, Latin America is currently being *decapitalized.*[30] Furthermore, the situation seems to be getting worse (see Whitehead, 1971: 220). In addition, Latin America does not receive trade preferences from the United States, such as Africa receives in West European markets, and foreign manpower is not an extremely critical item. There is a serious problem, however, in extending this analysis to Africa. Capital *is* necessary for economic development; the point is that, in the Latin American case, *foreign* capital may not be necessary because domestic resources may be sufficient–if properly used.

Perhaps it should be pointed out at this juncture that many Latin Americans are coming to realize that the only way that "proper" use of resources can be achieved is by "nationalizing" economic decision-making. There are several forms of national control currently being tried–i.e., the Peruvian, Chilean, and Cuban strategies. Two factors are common to all three strategies, although the Cubans have taken both further than the Chileans and Peruvians. First, at least the key sectors of the economy are being brought under state control. Second, some kind of serious consideration has been given to redistribution of income, both through eliminating excess consumption of the wealthiest groups and through increasing the consumption of the lower classes. The accompanying assumption is that the state itself can then provide the capital necessary to increase capacity through reinvestment of profits. In addition, the redistribution of income would increase domestic purchasing power, which would also lead to more growth. This does not mean, of course, that such problems as inflation, production, and foreign exchange bottlenecks will not occur, but only that the current problems involved in dependent development are seen as worse than the alternatives.

In most African countries, on the other hand, nationalizing every foreign dollar and sharply taxing the upper class still might not provide sufficient resources to stimulate development. For example, the median GDP in Africa in 1965 was only $296 million while in Latin America it was $1,170 million; means were $651 million for Africa and $4,377 million for Latin America. In other words, the median Latin American GDP was almost four times that of Africa, and the mean figure was almost seven times as great (figures were obtained by multiplying population by per capita GDP as given in Banks, 1970, for 1965). In addition, Africa's current lack of trained personnel might cause serious bottlenecks in the economies of many countries. The result, at best, could be very slow growth; at worst, it could be stagnation or even regression.[31] Under these circumstances, it is possible that an African leader might decide to continue to take advantage of foreign capital and manpower and preferential entry into European markets while they last and change strategy later. It is if this option is chosen that African countries would do well to look to Latin America to get some idea of potential problems caused by private capital exploitation, trade and industrialization, technology transfer, and distribution. Obviously, however, no direct answers can be provided because the situations in the two regions are dissimilar in many ways.

One final point suggested by current events in Latin America should also be seriously considered. Although it was suggested above that Africa might want to take advantage of foreign capital, trade preferences, and personnel, and then throw off such dependency relations after the benefits disappear, it is not entirely clear that such a change is possible. There are serious problems in each of the three such attempts in Latin America. Cuba succeeded in escaping from U.S. domination only at the cost of entering into a less than optimal relationship with the Soviet Union. Chile's new economic strategy is facing its most crucial year; whether Allende succeeds or not will be an important test which the rest of the Third World would do well to watch with care. Peru has "backslid" to the point of reopening such crucial areas as oil to foreign investment.

The question then is: does the choice of a development strategy at one point in time limit a country's options in the future? More specifically, does the decision to accept whatever short-run advantages there may be in dependency mean that future independent (interdependent) development is foreclosed? In trying to answer these questions, both the external links to the advanced countries, as well as the internal structure of classes and groups which benefit from these external relationships, must be considered. Furthermore, Third World countries are dealing not just with economic forces touched on in this paper, but also with cultural and political dependency, which are perhaps more powerful and insidious for being less obvious. Latin America can be said to have stumbled into dependency, lacking any precedents for guides. Africa, at least, has the opportunity to make an informed choice.

NOTES

1. There are now so many books and articles on dependency that it is impossible to cite them all. The works of the following authors have probably been the most influential up to this point: Fernando Henrique Cardoso, Theotonio Dos Santos, Enzo Faletto, Pablo González-Casanova, Anibal Quijano, Osvaldo Sunkel, and Francisco Weffort. Unfortunately, few of these works are translated into English. Two English-language readers containing articles on the subject are Fann and Hodges (1971) and Rhodes (1970). Two important unpublished papers in English are Bonilla (1971) and Sunkel (1971). A useful paper comparing dependency in Africa and Latin America after independence in both regions is Abernethy and Wirth (1967).

2. The phenomenon discussed under the rubric of dependency theory in the Latin American context is usually called neocolonialism with reference to Africa. Although the study of neocolonialism is less systematic, it deals with the same problems (see, for example, the discussion in Williams, 1970: 225-236).

3. The concept of "development" has been a particularly troublesome one for social scientists. Traditionally, economic development has been equated with growth (i.e., development as increasing capacity); more recently, however, distribution has been identified as an equally important aspect of economic development (i.e., development as increasing equality or some combination of capacity and equality). Thus, "failure to develop" means mere lack of growth for some countries; for others, it means distorted growth such that the aggregate GDP increases rapidly, but this increase is shared by only a small percentage of the population. The latter phenomenon has been called "dependent development" and is discussed more fully later in the article. For critiques of other theories of development from a dependency viewpoint see Bodenheimer (1971b), Dos Santos (1969), and Frank (1969: 21-94).

4. One of the main disagreements is over whether nation or class should be the basic unit of analysis (for an exchange on this controversy, see Cardoso, 1971b; Weffort, 1971).

5. Bodenheimer (1971a: 160-161) lists a series of characteristics of the international system and functions of Third World countries within this system which determine the forms of dependency at different times. The two forms most often

mentioned are (1) Third World nations as export economies primarily providing agricultural commodities and minerals with capital, technology, and industrial goods coming from the advanced countries, and (2) Third World nations as semi-industrialized economies (through import substitution) providing commodity markets and cheap labor. Technology and some capital continue to come from the advanced countries (see Cardoso, 1971a: 60-93; Dos Santos, 1971).

6. For a much longer list of indicators of economic dependency, see Green (1970: 289-290). Some of the indicators he uses are what I would consider preconditions for dependency; for example, exports and imports as a high percentage of GNP is a necessary precondition for the trade aspect of dependency to be relevant, but it does not represent dependency per se. Others of his indicators are repetitious, and I think the three used here are the most basic ones.

7. Obviously the documentation cannot all be listed here. Suffice it to say that the history of Cuba probably provides the most blatant examples of U.S. interference in the affairs of a Latin American country, ranging from landing the Marines at various times to manipulating the sugar quota to helping topple "undesirable" governments. But these events have occurred in other countries, too. Some recent examples are given in the concluding section of this paper. For a discussion of such interference in Africa, see Esseks (1971: 1067-1068).

8. Africa, in this paper, refers to "middle Africa," "tropical Africa," "black Africa" as it is varyingly known; that is, the independent countries south of the Sahara and north of the "battle line." These countries include Burundi, Cameroun, Central African Republic, Chad, Congo (Brazzaville), Congo (Kinshasa), Dahomey, Ethiopia, Gabon, Ghana, Guinea, Ivory Coast, Kenya, Liberia, Malagasy Republic, Malawi, Mali, Mauritania, Niger, Nigeria, Rwanda, Senegal, Sierra Leone, Somali Republic, Sudan, Tanzania, Togo, Uganda, Upper Volta, and Zambia. Latin American countries are the following twenty: Argentina, Bolivia, Brazil, Chile, Colombia, Costa Rica, Cuba, Dominican Republic, Ecuador, El Salvador, Guatemala, Haiti, Honduras, Mexico, Nicaragua, Panama, Paraguay, Peru, Uruguay, and Venezuela. Whenever possible, the tables in this paper were constructed so as to include *only* the above countries. Sometimes, however, others are included, such as the Portuguese colonies and the South African client states (though never South Africa itself nor the North African countries) in Africa, and Guyana and some of the French and British colonies in Latin America. The latter are not of sufficient importance, economically speaking, to affect the statistics a great deal.

9. For comparative figures on productivity for agriculture and industry in Latin America, see UN Economic Commission for Latin America (1969: 411). It should be noted also that current African development plans expect the agricultural sector to grow more slowly than industry (see, for example, the discussion in Robson and Lury, 1969: 37-38).

10. African countries included are Burundi, Dahomey, Ethiopia, Ghana, Guinea, Kenya, Liberia, Malagasy Republic, Nigeria, Rwanda, Sierra Leone, Tanzania, Togo, Uganda, and Zambia. Data are from U.S. Agency for International Development (1970a). All Latin American countries except Cuba are included in the Latin American statistics. Except for Peru and Uruguay, data are from U.S. Agency for International Development (1970b). Peruvian and Uruguayan data, as well as those for the donor countries, from United Nations (1969).

11. OECD countries include Austria, Belgium, Canada, Denmark, France, West Germany, Greece, Iceland, Ireland, Italy, Japan, Luxembourg, the Netherlands,

Norway, Portugal, Spain, Sweden, Switzerland, Turkey, the United Kingdom, and the United States.

12. There are several sources which discuss the history of foreign investment in Latin America. One which presents a fairly balanced appraisal is Diaz-Alejandro (1970). For a bibliography of Spanish sources on the subject, see Ffrench-Davis (1971).

13. U.S. investment percentages were calculated from U.S. Department of Commerce, *Survey of Current Business* for September of 1960, and September of 1967. Calculations for 1960 were based on the data given for East Africa, West Africa, and "other" under Central and South Africa (i.e., eliminating Rhodesia, Nyasaland, and the Union of South Africa). The "other" category among the investment sectors was considered to be agriculture. For 1967, calculations were based on Liberia and "other" (i.e., eliminating Libya and the Union of South Africa). The uncategorized investment in Liberia was considered as mining investment (iron). The "other" sectoral category was again taken as agriculture.

14. Historical accounts of U.S. aid before the Alliance for Progress are rare. See, for example, Gil (1971: esp. 215-219). Data on U.S. grants and loans to Latin America during the 1940s and 1950s can be found in U.S. Library of Congress (1959: 102-117, Tables V-VIII). The best account of the Alliance is found in Levinson and de Onis (1970).

15. Multilateral aid is partly loans and partly grants, although no exact breakdown could be found. World Bank Group money is all loans–most of it (the part from the IBRD) provided at commercial rates of about seven percent and a small part (from the IDA) on "soft terms" of about two percent. The regional bank money is also in loans, but most of the UN and EEC funds are grants.

16. The terms "gross" and "net" seem to be used somewhat loosely. For example, the OECD reports subtract only amortization payments, not interest, from gross bilateral loans to get a net figure. With multilateral aid (loans and grants), they subtract only subscriptions or contributions made to the agency but no interest or amortization. New investment does not include profit repatriation. Thus the "gross" figures in Table 6 are as follows: (1) gross investment–"net" investment taking no account of profits; (2) gross loans–nothing subtracted; (3) gross multilateral aid–same as net figures since no interest or amortization is taken out.

17. The Pearson figures for service payments include private as well as public loans. Private loans are not included in Table 6, and so are also missing in the "gross inflow" figures in Table 7, because of lack of data for Africa. Latin American private loans probably averaged about $450 million a year during the 1960s (this is an average of data from Furtado, 1970: 168-169; Whitehead, 1971: 216). If this figure is added to gross inflow and to the loan data for subtracting service payments, the net average outflow for Latin America drops from –$531 million to –$473 million. The already positive African figure would presumably be somewhat higher with private loans added.

18. African data back to 1958 are in the UN *Economic Commission for Africa Economic Bulletin* for June 1969; for Latin America, see UN Economic Commission for Latin America (1964: 136). See also comparisons for 1956 and 1965 in Jalée (1969: Tables V-5A and V-5B).

19. The figure 10,000 was arrived at as follows: Black Africa has approximately ten percent of total investment in underdeveloped countries (one-half of Africa's twenty percent). Therefore, it should have ten percent of the American technicians

or about 3,500. Since it is figured that Europe has about 65,000 investment personnel, black Africa should also have about ten percent of these, for a total of around 10,000.

20. Data are for 1965 and were calculated from information on population and number of doctors per million as reported in Taylor and Hudson (forthcoming).

21. Unfortunately, there are at least two problems with these tables. First, the gross inflow figure for 1955-1959 is copied incorrectly from Table 18.1 to 18.2; but this is easily corrected. Second, the data for profits from Venezuela are seriously wrong, based on every other source I have seen. I have estimated that rather than −$327 million, the figure is actually $609 million (based on IMF *Balance of Payments Yearbook* for 1955-1959, Volume 12, the section on Venezuela).

22. As might be expected, there is a controversy over how to measure the advantages and disadvantages of private investment. According to Charles Kindleberger (1969), one of the most articulate defenders of private foreign investment, calculations based merely on investment inflow and profit outflow are not adequate. Rather, one must also look at the export revenue produced by the investment, the tax revenue, and so on. None of these income sources would exist, he argues, without foreign investment. This argument is relevant, of course, in terms of new investment, but for already existing investment, the export advantages could be maintained by national control, and the profit outflow cut off. The question then becomes under what terms *new* investment is of sufficient importance to permit profit outflow to continue. The answers for Latin America and Africa may be different at the present time as discussed below.

23. There is accumulating evidence to show that the U.S. government and at least one private corporation (International Telephone and Telegraph) went further than just blocking aid to the new regime in Chile, but actually tried to prevent Allende from taking office. See the *New York Times* coverage beginning March 21, 1972, and Documentos secretos de la ITT (1972).

24. Perhaps the most formal relationship between the government and private foreign investors is the Investment Guarantee Program, where the U.S. government ensures corporations against expropriation, but only after the "host" countries have signed agreements saying that they will not confiscate property of U.S. nationals. The director of the Office of Regional Economic Policy admits that the threat of terminating aid was used to convince countries to sign the agreements (see McCamant, 1971: 28). According to a recent book by Teresa Hayter (1971), a strong relationship also exists between multilateral aid and private foreign investment.

25. The first such report was written in 1949 by Raúl Prebisch, former executive secretary of ECLA and published as the *Economic Development of Latin America and its Principal Problems* document E/CN.12/89/rev. 1. Most of the other reports by the trade division of ECLA touched on the same themes, up through Prebisch's final publication as executive secretary in 1963: *Toward a Dynamic Development Policy for Latin America,* document E/CN.12/680/rev. 1. Since then, ECLA has been less active.

26. Data for 1950 and 1957 can be found in Singer (1969: 129). The 1963 data are summarized in Adelman and Morris (1971). See discussion of these data in Cline (1971: 57-61).

27. The Brazilian estimates are based on income data in Fundacão Getulio Vargas (1971: 100-111). The increasing percentage of national income centered in São Paulo holds even when corrections for population change are applied. Compare 1940-1960

income data from above with population data in Brasil, Serviço Nacional de Recenseamento (1960: 3).

28. See discussion of stages as indicated in note 5. Data on returned value (linkages with local economy) for the oil industry in Venezuela can be found in Furtado (1970: 156) and for copper in Chile in Reynolds (1965).

29. The internal groups have been called the "infrastructure of dependency" by Bodenheimer (1971a: 162-165). See the accompanying discussion. This process currently can be seen in Chile as Allende tries to take control of the economy. The most striking example has probably been *El Mercurio,* a newspaper owned by a family closely tied into international financial circles, defending ITT and the CIA against charges that they tried to prevent Allende from taking office.

30. The situation, of course, varies from country to country. Venezuela is particularly important in this regard, having almost half of the private foreign investment in Latin America.

31. The best examples of these "worst" and "best" situations are probably Guinea in the early 1960s and Tanzania from the mid-1960s to the present. For discussions of these two countries in this context, see Berg (1964) for Guinea and Green (1970: 310-324) for Tanzania.

REFERENCES

ABERNETHY, D. and J. WIRTH (1967) "Dependence and development in new states: Latin America (1810-1850) and Africa (1957-67)." Stanford University Conference on Colonialism, Neocolonialism and Development. (unpublished)

ADELMAN, I. and C. T. MORRIS (1971) "An anatomy of patterns of income distribution in developing nations." Northwestern University. (unpublished)

AMIN, S. (1971) "Development and structural change: African experience," in B. Ward et al. (eds.) The Widening Gap: Development in the 1970's. New York: Columbia Univ. Press.

ANDERSON, C. (1970) "The changing international environment of development and Latin America in the 1970's." Interamerican Economic Affairs 24 (Autumn): 65-87.

ARRIGHI, G. (1970) "International corporations, labor aristocracies, and economic development in tropical Africa," pp. 220-267 in R. Rhodes (ed.) Imperialism and Underdevelopment. New York: Monthly Review Press.

BANKS, A. [ed.] (1970) Cross-Polity Time Series Data. Cambridge, Mass.: MIT Press.

BERG, E. (1964) "Socialism and economic development in tropical Africa." Q. J. of Economics 78: 549-573.

BLOCK, H. S. (1968) "Regional development finance," pp. 182-203 in R. Gardner and M. Millikan (eds.) The Global Partnership. New York: Praeger.

BODENHEIMER, S. (1971a) "Dependency and imperialism: the roots of Latin American underdevelopment," pp. 155-182 in K. T. Fann and D. Hodges (eds.) Readings in U.S. Imperialism. Boston: Porter Sargent.

--- (1971b) "The ideology of developmentalism: the American paradigm-surrogate for Latin American studies." Sage Professional Papers in Comparative Politics 2, 01-015.

BONILLA, F. (1971) "Elites and dependency." UCLA Conference on Dependence in Latin America. (unpublished)
Brasil, Serviço Nacional de Recenseamento (1960) Sinopse preliminar do censo demográfico. Rio de Janeiro: IBGE.
CARDOSO, F. H. (1971a) Ideologías de la burguesía industrial en sociedades dependientes. Mexico City: Siglo XXI.
--- (1971b) "¿'Teoría de dependencia' o análisis concreto de situaciones de dependencia? " Mexico City: Asociación de Becarios del Instituto de Investigaciones Sociales de la UNAM, DT-1.
CLINE, W. (1971) "The potential effects of income redistribution on economic growth in six Latin American countries." Princeton University. (unpublished)
DIAZ-ALEJANDRO, C. (1970) "Direct foreign investment in Latin America." Yale University Economic Growth Center Paper 150.
DOS SANTOS, T. (1971) "The structure of dependence," pp. 225-236 in K. T. Fann and D. Hodges (eds.) Readings in U.S. Imperialism. Boston: Porter Sargent.
--- (1969) "La crisis de la teoría del desarrollo y las relaciones de dependencia en América Latina," pp. 147-188 in H. Jaguaribe et al. (eds.) La dependencia político-económica de América Latina. Mexico City: Siglo XXI.
Education and World Affairs (1970) Modernization and the Migration of Talent. New York.
ESSEKS, J. (1971) "Economic dependency and political development in new states of Africa." J. of Politics 33 (November): 1052-1075.
FANN, K. T. and D. HODGES [eds.] (1971) Readings in U.S. Imperialism. Boston: Porter Sargent.
FFRENCH-DAVIS, R. (1971) La inversión extranjera en América Latina: tendencias recientes y perspectivas. Santiago: CEPLAN.
FISHLOW, A. (1971) "The Brazilian size distribution of income." University of California, Berkeley. (unpublished)
FRANK, A. G. (1969) Latin America: Underdevelopment or Revolution. New York: Monthly Review Press.
FRIEDMAN, W. et al. (1966) International Financial Aid. New York: Columbia Univ. Press.
Fundacão Getulio Vargas (1971) "Estimativa da renda interna segundo ramos de actividades por unidades da Federacão." Conjuntura Econômica 25 (September): 100-111.
FURTADO, C. (1970) Economic Development in Latin America. Cambridge, Eng.: Cambridge Univ. Press.
GIL, F. (1971) Latin American-United States Relations. New York: Harcourt-Brace-Jovanovich.
GOLDMAN, M. (1967) Soviet Foreign Aid. New York: Praeger.
GORDON, W. (1968) "Has foreign aid been overstated? " Interamerican Economic Affairs 21 (Spring): 3-18.
--- (1965) The Political Economy of Latin America. New York: Columbia Univ. Press.
GREEN, R. (1970) "Political independence and the national economy of decolonialization," pp. 273-324 in C. Allen and R. W. Johnson (eds.) African Perspectives. Cambridge, Eng.: Cambridge Univ. Press.
GREY, C. (1969) Resource Flows to Less-Developed Countries. New York: Praeger.

GRUNWALD, J. et al. (1971) Latin American Economic Integration and the United States. Washington D.C.: Brookings Institution.

HAYTER, T. (1971) Aid as Imperialism. Middlesex, Eng.: Penguin.

HELLEINER, G. (1971) "Structural change in Africa," in B. Ward et al. (eds.) The Widening Gap: Development in the 1970's. New York: Columbia Univ. Press.

HERRERA, A. O. et al. (1970) América Latina: ciencia y tecnología en el desarrollo de la sociedad. Santiago: Editorial Universitaria.

HIRSCHMAN, A. O. (1969) "The political economy of import-substituting industrialization in Latin America," pp. 237-266 in C. Nisbit (ed.) Latin America: Problems of Economic Development. New York: Free Press.

--- [ed.] (1961) Latin American Issues: Essays and Comments. New York: Twentieth Century Fund.

HUNTER, G. (1963) Education for a Developing Region. London: Institute for Race Relations.

ILLICH, I. (1969) "Outwitting the 'developed' countries." New York Rev. of Books 13 (November): 20-24.

ITT (1972) Documentos secretos. Santiago: Empresa Editoria Nacional Quimantu.

JALEE, P. (1969) The Third World in World Economy. New York: Monthly Review Press.

--- (1968) The Pillage of the Third World. New York: Monthly Review Press.

KAMARCK, A. (1971) The Economics of African Development. New York: Praeger.

KINDLEBERGER, C. (1969) American Business Abroad: Six Lectures on Direct Investment. New Haven, Conn.: Yale Univ. Press.

KIRDAR, U. (1966) The Structure of United Nations Economic Aid to Underdeveloped Countries. The Hague: Martinus Nijhoff.

LESSA, C. (1969) "De la constitución actual del capitalismo dependiente," pp. 52-90 in C. Lessa and T. Vasconi (eds.) Hacia una crítica de las interpretaciones del desarrollo latinoamericano. Caracas: CENDES.

LEVINSON, J. and J. DE ONIS (1970) The Alliance that Lost its Way. Chicago: Quadrangle.

McCAMANT, J. (1971) "Two faces of foreign aid: cooperation and imperialism." International Studies Association/West Conference. (unpublished)

MADDISON, A. (1970) Economic Progress and Policy in Developing Countries. London: George Allen & Unwin.

--- (1965) Foreign Skills and Technical Assistance in Economic Development. Paris: OECD.

MAGDOFF, H. (1969) The Age of Imperialism. New York: Monthly Review Press.

El Mercurio (1972) Santiago, Chile.

MULLER, K. (1967) The Foreign Aid Programs of the Soviet Bloc and Communist China. New York: Walker.

New York Times (1971-1972).

North American Congress for Latin America (1972) The New Chile. Berkeley, Calif.: NACLA.

Organization for Economic Cooperation and Development (series a). Development Assistance, 1960-1970.

--- (series b) The Flow of Financial Resources to Less-Developed Countries, 1956-1963, 1961-1965.

--- (series c) The Geographical Distribution of Financial Flows to Less-Developed Countries, 1960-1964, 1965, 1966-1967.

--- (series d) Technical Assistance and the Needs of Developing Countries, 1968.

OSTRANDER, F. T. (1969) "U.S. private investment in Africa." Africa Report 14, 7: 38-41.

PEARSON, L. et al. (1969) Partners in Development. New York: Praeger.

POWELSON, J. (1964) Latin America: Today's Economic and Social Revolution. New York: McGraw-Hill.

REYNOLDS, C. (1965) "Development problems of an export economy," pp. 203-398 in M. Mamalakis and C. Reynolds (eds.) Essays on the Chilean Economy. Homewood, Ill.: Richard D. Irwin.

RHODES, R. [ed.] (1970) Imperialism and Underdevelopment. New York: Monthly Review Press.

ROBSON, P. and D. A. LURY [eds.] (1969) The Economies of Africa. Evanston, Ill.: Northwestern Univ. Press.

RUSSETT, B. et al. [eds.] (1964) World Handbook of Political and Social Indicators. New Haven, Conn.: Yale Univ. Press.

SAWYER, C. (1966) Communist Trade with Developing Countries, 1955-1965. New York: Praeger.

SCHEUCH, E. (1966) "Cross-national comparisons using aggregate data: some substantive and methodological problems," pp. 131-168 in R. Merritt and S. Rokkan (eds.) Comparing Nations. New Haven, Conn.: Yale Univ. Press.

SCHMITTER, P. (1971) Interest Conflict and Political Change in Brazil. Stanford, Calif.: Stanford Univ. Press.

SEIDMAN, A. (1970) "Old motives, new methods: foreign enterprise in Africa today," pp. 251-272 in C. Allen and R. W. Johnson (eds.) African Perspectives. Cambridge, Eng.: Cambridge Univ. Press.

SINGER, M. (1969) Growth, Equality and the Mexican Experience. Austin: Univ. of Texas Press.

SUNKEL, O. (1971) "Transnational capitalism and national disintegration in Latin America." UCLA Conference on Dependence in Latin America. (unpublished)

--- (1970) "La universidad latinoamericana ante el avance científico y técnico." Estudios Internacionales 13 (April-June): 60-89.

--- and P. PAZ (1970) El subdesarrollo latinoamericano y la teoría del desarrollo. Mexico City: Siglo XXI.

TANSKY, L. (1967) U.S. and U.S.S.R. Aid to Developing Countries. New York: Praeger.

TANZER, M. (1969) The Political Economy of International Oil and the Underdeveloped Countries. Boston: Beacon.

TAYLOR, C. and M. HUDSON [eds.] (forthcoming) World Handbook of Political and Social Indicators. New Haven, Conn.: Yale Univ. Press.

UNCTAD (1967) Crecimiento, financiación del desarrollo y ayuda: informe sobre créditos condicionados: Chile.

United Nations (series) International Flow of Long-Term Capital and Official Donations, 1959-1961, 1960-1962, 1961-1965, 1961-1966, 1962-1966, 1964-1968.

--- (1969) Yearbook of National Account Statistics.

--- (1968) Yearbook of International Trade Statistics.

--- Economic Commission for Africa (series) Economic Bulletin for Africa, 1960-1970.

--- (1969a) Economic Conditions in Africa in Recent Years.

——— (1969b) Flow of Resources to Africa.
——— (1967) A Survey of Economic Conditions in Africa.

United Nations, Economic Commission for Latin America (series a) Economic Bulletin for Latin America, 1950-1970.

——— (series b) Economic Survey of Latin America, 1950-1970.

——— (1964) The Economic Development of Latin America in the Postwar Years.

U.S. Agency for International Development (1970a) AID Economic Data Book: Africa 1970.

——— (1970b) AID Economic Data Book: Latin America 1970.

——— (1967) AID Economic Data Book: Latin America 1967.

U.S. Department of Commerce (series) Survey of Current Business, 1960-67.

U.S. Library of Congress (1959) Legislative Reference Service. U.S. Foreign Aid. Eighty-sixth Congress, House Document 116.

VELIZ, C. (1968) Latin America and the Caribbean: A Handbook. New York: Praeger.

WARD, B. et al. [eds.] (1971) The Widening Gap: Development in the 1970's. New York: Columbia Univ. Press.

WEFFORT, F. (1971) "Notas sobre la 'teoría de la dependencia': ¿teoría de clases o ideología nacional? " Mexico City: Asociación de Becarios del Instituto de Investigaciones Sociales de la UNAM, DT-1.

WHITEHEAD, L. (1971) "The trade and aid relationship in Latin America," in B. Ward et al. (eds.) The Widening Gap: Development in the 1970's. New York: Columbia Univ. Press.

WILKIE, J. (1967) The Mexican Revolution: Federal Expenditure and Social Change since 1910. Berkeley: Univ. of California Press.

WILLIAMS, G. (1970) "The social stratification of a neo-colonial economy," pp. 225-250 in C. Allen and R. W. Johnson (eds.) African Perspectives. Cambridge, Eng.: Cambridge Univ. Press.

YATES, P. L. (1959) Forty Years of Foreign Trade. London: George Allen & Unwin.

APPENDIX

APPENDIX

ECONOMIC INDICATORS FOR AFRICAN, LATIN AMERICAN, AND MAJOR DONOR COUNTRIES, 1965

	GNP Per Capita	Agriculture as % of GDP	Industry as % of GDP	Railroad Miles/ Square Mile	Energy Consumed, kg Per Capita of Coal Equivalent
AFRICA					
Burundi	$ 43	60	—	0	12
Cameroun	139	37	11	1.7	71
Central African Republic	136	49	12	0	38
Chad	136	54	4	0	15
Congo (Brazzaville)	201	23	17	2.3	148
Congo (Kinshasa)	130	22	16	3.5	83
Dahomey	77	46	3	8.1	30
Ethiopia	50	64	7	1.4	10
Gabon	356	23	6	0	240
Ghana	259	51	19	8.5	104
Guinea	53	54	3	4.3	98
Ivory Coast	250	34	9	3.2	152
Kenya	105	35	11	9.1	124
Liberia	202	25	5	5.5	259
Malagasy Republic	111	32	11	2.3	42
Malawi	48	47	5	4.8	42
Mali	75	54	6	0.8	21
Mauritania	117	38	1	1.0	48
Niger	87	62	—	0	13
Nigeria	73	56	7	5.2	44
Rwanda	41	69	14	0	15
Senegal	223	33	14	3.1	145
Sierra Leone	149	31	6	12.9	68
Somali Republic	75	—	—	0	27
Sudan	101	54	6	3.4	69
Tanzania	73	54	5	4.3	51
Togo	103	45	5	12.5	41
Uganda	90	59	8	4.5	42
Upper Volta	50	58	2	3.7	10
Zambia	228	10	8	1.7	487
Median	$ 104	47	7	3.2	44
Range	$41-$356	10-69	1-19	0-12.9	10-487

APPENDIX (continued)

LATIN AMERICA					
Argentina	$ 705	17	37	29.6	1341
Bolivia	156	23	28	5.1	185
Brazil	149	29	28	6.3	347
Chile	637	10	26	17.8	1089
Colombia	231	32	22	4.8	532
Costa Rica	409	31	15	25.0	306
Cuba	259	—	—	481.2	950
Dominican Republic	210	24	18	41.8	194
Ecuador	216	34	21	10.0	212
El Salvador	296	32	16	58.6	168
Guatemala	296	28	16	17.1	182
Haiti	87	49	—	23.3	33
Honduras	237	44	17	15.3	151
Mexico	465	17	32	19.3	977
Nicaragua	346	35	16	5.0	234
Panama	484	24	18	4.5	1115
Paraguay	227	38	16	4.5	126
Peru	270	20	25	4.2	588
Uruguay	625	16	26	26.4	916
Venezuela	874	28	40	1.5	2974
Median	$ 296	28	22	16.2	326
Range	$87-$874	10-49	15-40	1.5-481.2	33-2974
DONOR COUNTRIES					
France	$1,870	5	38	112.2	2951
Germany (West)	1,907	5	45	229.0	4234
Soviet Union	1,382	22	52	9.4	3611
United Kingdom	1,833	3	41	96.8	5151
United States	3,482	4	34	58.3	9201
Median	$1,870	8	41	96.8	4234
Range	$1,382-$3,482	3-21	34-52	9.4-229.0	2951-9201

APPENDIX (continued)

	% Literate,[a] Age 15 Plus	Higher Education, Students/10,000 Population	% GNP[b] Growth Rate	% Per Capita[b] Growth Rate
AFRICA				
Burundi	–	1	1.9	–0.1
Cameroun	10	3	2.8	0.6
Central African Republic	15	0	1.5	–1.0
Chad	5	0	0.9	–0.6
Congo (Brazzaville)	23	11	3.2	1.7
Congo (Kinshasa)	35	2	1.6	–0.5
Dahomey	5	0	3.1	0.2
Ethiopia	5	1	4.7	2.7
Gabon	8	1	4.3	3.5
Ghana	23	5	2.6	–0.1
Guinea	10	2	5.3	2.5
Ivory Coast	20	4	8.4	5.4
Kenya	23	3	4.0	1.1
Liberia	10	7	3.2	1.5
Malagasy Republic	35	5	1.9	–0.5
Malawi	8	1	5.7	3.2
Mali	5	1	2.8	0.7
Mauritania	3	0	8.9	6.9
Niger	3	0	3.1	0.1
Nigeria	33	2	3.5	1.1
Rwanda	8	0	4.9	1.7
Senegal	8	8	2.3	–0.1
Sierra Leone	10	4	2.6	1.3
Somali Republic	5	0	2.4	–1.6
Sudan	13	6	3.1	0.2
Tanzania	18	1	4.4	1.9
Togo	8	0	3.1	0.5
Uganda	25	2	3.7	1.2
Upper Volta	8	0	1.6	–0.6
Zambia	41	0	4.6	1.6
Median	10	1	3.1	0.9
Range	3-41	0-11	0.9-8.9	–1.6-6.9

APPENDIX (continued)

LATIN AMERICA				
Argentina	91	109	−0.1	−1.7
Bolivia	32	36	4.9	3.4
Brazil	61	19	4.7	1.5
Chile	84	51	3.5	1.0
Colombia	65	21	4.4	2.1
Costa Rica	84	50	6.0	1.9
Cuba	75	40	–	–
Dominican Republic	65	18	1.6	−1.4
Ecuador	67	30	4.0	0.8
El Salvador	49	12	6.6	3.3
Guatemala	38	17	6.1	2.8
Haiti	10	4	1.0	−1.3
Honduras	45	11	4.0	0.7
Mexico	65	31	6.2	3.0
Nicaragua	50	20	8.3	4.6
Panama	73	66	8.0	4.7
Paraguay	68	19	3.5	1.0
Peru	61	42	6.6	3.0
Uruguay	90	61	0.2	−1.0
Venezuela	80	54	5.0	1.5
Median	65	31	4.7	1.5
Range	10-91	4-109	0.1-8.3	−1.7-4.7
DONOR COUNTRIES				
France	99	104	5.0	3.5
Germany (West)	99	63	4.7	3.4
Soviet Union	99	167	6.4	5.0
United Kingdom	99	49	3.3	2.5
United States	99	284	4.6	3.2
Median	99	104	4.7	3.4
Range	99	49-284	3.3-6.4	2.5-5.0

APPENDIX (continued)

	Population 000's	% in Cities Over 50,000	Imports-Exports as % of GNP	Gini Index (income)	Gini Index (land)
AFRICA					
Burundi	3,210	2.2	—	—	—
Cameroun	5,229	5.3	43.4	—	—
Central African Republic	1,352	10.0	44.3	—	—
Chad	3,307	2.7	24.5	.32	—
Congo (Brazzaville)	840	24.5	81.2	—	—
Congo (Kinshasa)	15,627	14.0	51.0	—	—
Dahomey	2,365	6.3	29.1	.52	—
Ethiopia	22,600	3.4	26.3	—	—
Gabon	463	0	121.5	.64	—
Ghana	7,740	12.9	33.5	—	—
Guinea	3,500	3.6	38.7	—	—
Ivory Coast	3,835	8.8	53.4	.49	—
Kenya	9,365	5.6	46.6	.50	.69
Liberia	1,070	7.3	112.2	—	—
Malagasy Republic	6,420	6.1	39.8	.50	—
Malawi	3,940	2.7	53.0	—	—
Mali	4,576	3.6	19.9	—	.48
Mauritania	1,050	0	56.4	—	—
Niger	3,328	0	25.2	.31	—
Nigeria	57,500	4.2	31.4	.51	—
Rwanda	3,110	0	22.6	—	—
Senegal	3,490	10.8	42.9	.58	—
Sierra Leone	2,290	5.6	80.5	.56	—
Somali Republic	2,500	5.7	58.7	—	—
Sudan	13,540	4.2	29.7	.41	—
Tanzania	10,515	4.0	42.1	.46	—
Togo	1,638	4.8	46.2	—	—
Uganda	7,551	1.0	44.5	—	—
Upper Volta	4,858	2.8	24.2	—	—
Zambia	3,710	2.5	108.2	—	—
Median	3,750	4.2	43.4	.48	.59
Range	463-57,500	0-24.5	19.9-121.5	.31-.64	.48-.69

APPENDIX (continued)

LATIN AMERICA					
Argentina	22,352	32.0	15.7	.42	.87
Bolivia	3,697	20.3	37.9	.49	—
Brazil	82,222	24.8	12.3	.54	.85
Chile	8,567	26.1	26.7	.44	—
Colombia	18,068	32.8	19.5	.62	.86
Costa Rica	1,433	23.7	49.0	.51	.78
Cuba	7,631	37.0	51.7	—	—
Dominican Republic	3,619	12.6	23.3	—	.80
Ecuador	5,084	26.2	28.7	.32	.86
El Salvador	2,928	19.0	49.1	.52	.83
Guatemala	4,438	15.1	29.5	—	.86
Haiti	4,396	5.9	22.0	—	—
Honduras	2,284	12.0	52.2	—	.76
Mexico	42,689	21.0	13.9	.52	.69
Nicaragua	1,655	24.8	54.5	—	.80
Panama	1,300	33.5	45.6	.48	.74
Paraguay	2,030	15.3	23.7	—	—
Peru	11,650	23.8	32.5	.61	.93
Uruguay	2,715	49.8	22.0	—	.83
Venezuela	8,722	39.1	53.4	.35	.91
Median	4,417	24.5	29.1	.50	.83
Range	1,300-82,222	5.9-49.8	12.3-54.5	.32-.62	.69-.93
DONOR COUNTRIES					
France	48,922	25.0	21.7	.52	—
Germany (West)	58,041	37.0	31.5	.47	.67
Soviet Union	230,600	35.0	,9.8	—	—
United Kingdom	54,595	48.6	29.1	.40	.72
United States	194,572	36.3	7.3	.40	.71
Median	58,041	36.3	21.7	.45	.71
Range	48,922-230,600	25.0-48.€	7.3-31.5	.40-.52	.67-.72

Notes to Appendix

SOURCES: GNP per capita—Banks (1970: 269-282); agriculture and industry as percentage of GDP—Kamarck (1971) for African countries, Taylor and Hudson (forthcoming: Table 5-11) for Latin American and donor countries; railroad mileage—Banks (1970: 99-136); energy consumption—Banks (1970: 255-268); literacy—Taylor and Hudson (forthcoming: Table 4-5); higher education—Banks (1970: 207-236); GNP growth rate—Kamarck (1971: 56-57) for African countries, Veliz (1968) for Latin American countries, Taylor and Hudson (forthcoming: Tables 5-4 and 5-5) for donor countries; population—Taylor and Hudson (forthcoming: Table 5-1); urbanization—Banks (1970: 55-98); trade as percentage of GNP—Taylor and Hudson (forthcoming: Table 6-7); Gini indices for income—Adelman and Morris (1971) for African and Latin American countries, U.N. Economic Commission for Latin America (1969: 388), Russett et al. (1964: 245) for donor countries; Gini indices for land—Taylor and Hudson (forthcoming: Table 4-14).

a. Literacy data are for population aged fifteen and above except for the following: Argentina and Senegal (fourteen and above), Bolivia (five and above), Brazil (ten and above), Peru (seventeen and above), and Zambia (seven and above).

b. Growth rate for African and Latin American countries is based on the period 1961-1967; for donor countries the period is 1960-1965.

BARBARA STALLINGS is a graduate student in comparative politics at Stanford University. She is currently a Foreign Area Fellow, doing dissertation research in Chile on economic development strategies of the Alessandri, Frei, and Allende regimes. She has also published "Los intelectuales en la política mexicana," Aportes, *October 1972.*